101
FUSS-FREE BAKES

DEDICATION
Jessica Born

7 June 1990 – 28 January 2009

Jessica Born loved to bake, using her much-loved first edition of *101 Fuss-Free Bakes* to make cakes, muffins and biscuits for her family. After matriculating at the end of 2008, she was set to go to university but only had two concerns: her cat, and where she would bake. Sadly, Jessica died suddenly in January 2009. To her mother, Liddy, *101 Fuss-Free Bakes* is a constant reminder of the fun Jessica had in the kitchen, and in it she finds great comfort, as each recipe brings back many happy memories.

101 FUSS-FREE BAKES

HILARY BILLER • JENNY KAY • ELINOR STORKEY

ACKNOWLEDGEMENTS

The recipes featured in this book are a collection we have gathered over the years.

Many of the recipes have appeared in the *The Star* newspaper's Angela Day column and we thank them for the permission to use these recipes.

The Sweet Wine Grape Cake on page 67 is courtesy of Phillippa Cheifitz and we thank her for giving us permission to publish it.

Without the support of Random House Struik and their wonderful team, this book would not have been possible. A big thank you to Linda de Villiers, Beverley Dodd and Bronwen Leak.

Thank you to stylist Lisa Clark and photographer Christoph Heierli – the images are truly beautiful.

HILARY BILLER, JENNY KAY, ELINOR STORKEY

HILARY BILLER

Hilary was *The Star's* 'Angela Day' for over 11 years before joining *The Sunday Times* as food editor. She is widely respected for her accessible and innovative approach to cooking, and has twice been the recipient of the prestigious Galliova Award and named South Africa's food writer of the year. She is the author of *The Step-by-Step Cookbook* and *Great Meals Fast*, and co-author of *Braai* – all published by Struik Lifestyle.

JENNY KAY

Jenny has worked in the food industry for more than 25 years, with baking and teaching playing an important role. She is currently *The Star's* 'Angela Day' and co-author of *Braai*, published by Struik Lifestyle, and *Angela Day Favourites*, published by *The Star*. Jenny is a perfectionist when it comes to baking and strives to make all her recipes accessible and user-friendly.

ELINOR STORKEY

Passionate about baking, Elinor has spent the past 30 years in the food industry. She holds an advanced cordon bleu certificate from London and is a versatile member of *The Star's* Angela Day team, developing recipes, assisting with cookery classes and demonstrations, and answering reader queries. Elinor is also co-author of *Braai*, published by Struik Lifestyle, and *Angela Day Favourites*, published by *The Star*.

CONTENTS

INTRODUCTION

Why a book on baking? In an era when more people work full time, time is at a premium, spending power is diminished and ready-made options are so tempting, successful home baking is more important than ever. That's why a collection of tried and tested ideas that won't see you spending hours in the kitchen is so worthwhile.

Unlike cooking, baking is a science, and the correct proportions of ingredients are essential for a successful end product. Many people may think the art of baking is the epitome of nutritional frivolity, but a life without the occasional home-baked product would be so much poorer!

Trying a new recipe for the first time can be an interesting and rewarding experience or a disappointing and intimidating one. We believe in home baking – you just can't beat the home-made brand and that's why we have put together a collection of easy recipes to add to your repertoire. All have been triple tested to guarantee success; however, just remember that, for good results, there are a few simple rules to follow.

KNOW YOUR INGREDIENTS

FLOUR

It is imperative to use the correct type of flour for the recipe. The majority of our recipes use cake flour, which is manufactured from soft wheat and comes from the whitest part of the kernel. Cake flour contains less gluten – the protein constituent of the wheat kernel – and is therefore used for most confectionery baking. It's often just referred to as flour or as cake flour.

Self-raising flour is cake flour to which a raising agent, such as baking powder, has already been added.

Wholewheat flour is made from white bread flour to which wheaten bran is added. Its high fibre content makes it a good choice for a more healthy baked product. Wholewheat flour tends to absorb more liquid.

Use flour before the sell-by date and store in an airtight container. For prolonged storage, store flour in the fridge or the freezer.

SUGAR

White sugar, brown sugar (light, dark and sticky) and castor sugar are commonly used in baking.

Castor sugar has a fine texture, enabling it to cream easily.

Brown sugar gives a baked product a good colour and pleasant flavour.

Icing sugar is not suitable for use in flour mixtures because it contains cornflour, which will cause lumps and give the baking a heavy texture.

EGGS

Eggs add colour and flavour to baking. They give the product structure and act as a raising agent. Baking is best done with fresh eggs that are at room temperature. To test if an egg is fresh, gently drop it into a beaker of tap water. If the eggs sinks it is fresh and if it floats it is past its sell-by date. All the recipes call for extra-large eggs (65 g).

FAT

All the recipes in this book call for butter because that is our baking preference. It has an excellent flavour and improves the quality of the baked product. Margarine can be substituted, but it is essential to use brick margarine and not the tub variety for baking success.

BAKING PANS

Using the correct baking pans will go a long way towards achieving success. It is important to measure the size of the pan accurately using the INSIDE measurement. The wrong size can result in a cake either not being the correct height or the mixture overflowing.

Baking pans come in various shapes and sizes from round, tube and square to rectangular, and they can be deep, shallow or loose-bottom. Standard sizes for round and loose-bottom pans are 18 cm, 20 cm, 22 cm, 23 cm and 24 cm; larger sizes are normally speciality tins. Square pans are usually available as 20 cm, 22 cm and 24 cm. Tube or bundt pans are 20 cm, 23 cm, 24 cm and 25 cm. A lamington or brownie pan measures 27 x 17.5 x 3 cm.

Muffin pans come in three sizes: mini, standard and extra large. Standard pans consist of 12 cups and extra-large pans have 6 cups. Also available are mini loaf pans, which are ideal for baking individual loaves.

A chiffon pan is a loose-bottom, deep ring pan with three legs extending above the edge of the tin. It is essential that a cooked chiffon cake is immediately inverted onto these legs and left to cool completely in the pan. Cooling in this suspended position creates the correct light texture characteristic of a chiffon cake.

If your pans are not coated with a teflon coating, they are more likely to rust and will require a little more care: dry completely before packing away. A good idea is to wash and dry the pan and place it in the now switched-off oven where the residual warmth will dry it completely. Pans can be wiped with sunflower oil if not used regularly. If rust does appear, it can be removed with a scourer and then coated with a thin film of oil.

Teflon-coated pans do not normally rust. Any scouring or scraping with a sharp utensil will remove the coating.

Different containers, such as cardboard boxes, can also be used for baking. An empty beer box is ideal to use for baking a large cake or a fruitcake. It measures 27 x 40 cm. A note of caution: the boxes are usually secured with glue and need to be stapled in the corners and lined with foil before using.

Glass containers can also be used for baking, but they are not ideal as glass is not a good conductor of heat and uneven baking may occur. In addition, baking in glass does not give the characteristic golden–brown colour of a baked product.

PREPARING BAKING PANS

There are three ways of preparing a pan before baking: smear with butter or margarine, lightly coat with flour, or coat with a non-stick cooking spray. The latter is the easiest and most common form of preparing a tin. To make sure that nothing will ever stick to the base of your tin, you can choose to line the base with a piece of baking or greaseproof paper. Wax paper is not suitable as it disintegrates as the heat melts the wax coating. Some recipes in this book also call for the base and sides of a pan to be lined with baking paper.

INTRODUCTION

BAKING Q&A

IS IT NECESSARY TO SIFT DRY INGREDIENTS?

Sifting aerates flour and gives a more uniform texture, so it is a good idea to get into the habit of sifting. Sifting disperses dry ingredients evenly and breaks up any lumps, especially in ingredients like cocoa powder and icing sugar.

I'VE RUN OUT OF BAKING POWDER. IS THERE ANY SUBSTITUTE?

Baking powder is a combination of cream of tartar and bicarbonate of soda. For 15 ml of baking powder, combine 10 ml cream of tartar and 5 ml bicarbonate of soda.

WHAT WILL HAPPEN IF I SUBSTITUTE MARGARINE FOR BUTTER IN BAKING?

There will be a difference in flavour. Butter is the better option, but block margarine can be used instead. Never use tub margarine because it will not work.

CAN I USE OIL INSTEAD OF BUTTER?

If a recipe calls for creaming, oil is not ideal as it gives a coarse texture. However, where air is added by means of beaten eggs, oil can be used in equal proportions as called for in the recipe.

MUST I LINE A CAKE PAN?

With today's non-stick baking pans and spray, lining is almost a thing of the past. For peace of mind, however, line cake pans, especially the base, to ensure the cakes slip out easily without breaking. Line pans with baking or greaseproof paper, not wax paper.

WHY DOES A CAKE RISE TO A POINT?

The mixture was beaten too much, the batter was too stiff, the oven temperature was too high or the cake pan was too deep.

MY CAKE CRUST IS CRACKED. WHY?

The oven temperature was too high at the start of baking. The batter could have been too stiff and the cake pan too deep.

THE CAKE HAS FALLEN IN THE CENTRE. WHY?

The batter was too thin. The proportions of sugar, fat, raising agent or liquid were too high. The oven temperature was too low or the oven door was opened too soon and the cake could have been removed before it was cooked.

MY CAKE IS PERFECT EXCEPT FOR THE SPECKLED CRUST. WHAT WENT WRONG?

The sugar was too coarse and did not dissolve properly. The mixture could have been overbeaten, causing the air bubbles to dry out on the surface.

INTRODUCTION

WHY IS THE CAKE HEAVY AND SUGARY?

The ingredients were incorrectly mixed and the sugar or raising agent quantity is too high.

WHAT CAUSES MUFFINS TO BE MISSHAPEN WITH TUNNELS AND HOLES?

The batter was overmanipulated, the raising agent was not equally distributed or the oven temperature was too high.

WHY DO MY SCONES TURN OUT FLAT AND HEAVY?

The dough was manipulated too much and flattened before cutting out. The oven temperature was too low and the scones did not bake through.

HOW DO I TELL IF A CAKE IS COOKED?

Your cake will be ready when it looks and smells done. In most cases, the cake shrinks away from the sides of the cake pan and when the top of the cake is pressed lightly with a finger, it springs back. If a thin metal skewer is inserted into the thickest part of the cake and it comes out clean and shiny, your cake should be cooked.

HOW DO I KNOW IF MY OVEN IS AT THE CORRECT TEMPERATURE?

To check the true temperature in your oven, place an oven thermometer (available from most kitchen speciality stores) on the middle shelf of the oven. Switch on the oven and, when the indicator light goes off, check and see if the thermometer has the same reading as the temperature you had set it to. If not, and before you call in a professional, retry the experiment. If it is still inaccurate, have the oven thermostat checked by a professional or, if the difference is minor, simply readjust the temperature according to the discrepancy. Remember that if the element in the oven comes on for any length of time during the baking period, this could indicate a problem with the thermostat.

IS THERE A DIFFERENCE BETWEEN BAKING IN A THERMOFAN OVEN AS OPPOSED TO A CONVENTIONAL ELEMENT OVEN?

In a thermofan oven, the heat is distributed by a fan (usually in the back of the oven). This means the heat is evenly distributed throughout the oven, allowing the baking of more than one item at a time. Thermofan ovens often tend to have a hot spot and, once you have identified it, you can move the baked items around to achieve a more even result. Some manufacturers recommend a reduction of 10 °C when baking in a thermofan oven. In a conventional element oven, the heat is generated by a top and bottom element and therefore baking can only take place on the middle shelf.

INTRODUCTION

TIPS FOR SUCCESS EVERY TIME

- Choose the recipe you like and always read it through carefully first. Check that you have all the ingredients on hand.
- Use ingredients at room temperature and make sure you have enough time on your hands and are free of interruptions or distractions to produce that perfect bake.
- Remember, too, that no matter how accurate you think your oven is, no two ovens give the same result. Nor are the ingredients uniform in the way they behave. The absorbency of flour, for instance, depends on its freshness and on the humidity of your kitchen.
- The correct baking temperature is important, so set the oven to the required temperature before beginning.
- Prepare the correct baking pans.
- Always follow the same units of measurement throughout a recipe. We have used millilitres for the majority of ingredients – both liquid and dry (because a set of measuring cups is accessible to most bakers) – except for butter and ingredients such as nuts.

METRIC MADE EASY

250 ml = 1 cup
125 ml = 1/2 cup
80 ml = 1/3 cup
60 ml = 1/4 cup
5 ml = 1 teaspoon
2.5 ml = 1/2 teaspoon
15 ml = 1 tablespoon
10 ml = 1 dessertspoon

Some useful conversions – weight equivalent equal to 250 ml (1 cup):
butter = 250 g
cocoa = 100 g
coconut = 80 g
currants and raisins = 150 g
custard powder = 130 g
dates, chopped = 150 g
cake flour = 140 g
oats = 90 g
sugar, brown = 200 g
sugar, castor = 210 g
sugar, white = 200 g
sugar, icing = 130 g

INTRODUCTION

BAKING AT ALTITUDE

Altitude can also play a part in the success of a recipe. All our recipes have been tested at high altitude. Here is a guide to baking recipes at sea level:

- Increase the baking powder: increase by 1–2 ml for every 5 ml called for.
- Increase the sugar: increase the sugar by 15–30 ml per 250 ml called for.
- Decrease the liquid: reduce the liquid 15–30 ml per 250 ml called for.
- Decrease the flour: decrease 15 ml of flour per 250 ml called for.
- Lower the baking temperature by 10 °C.

INTRODUCTION

BREADS

RUSTIC ROSEMARY FLATBREAD

500 ml flour

30 ml chopped fresh rosemary

5 ml baking powder

5 ml salt

80 ml olive oil, plus more for brushing

125-150 ml water

sea salt flakes for sprinkling

Preheat the oven to 200 °C with a heavy baking sheet on the middle rack.

Combine the flour, chopped rosemary, baking powder and salt in a mixing bowl. Stir and make a well in the centre. Add the oil and enough water to form a dough. Knead the dough gently on a floured work surface. Divide the dough into three pieces. Keep one aside and wrap the remaining pieces in plastic wrap. On a lightly floured surface, roll the unwrapped piece into a thin, round rustic shape. Lightly brush the top with olive oil and sprinkle with salt. Slide the flatbread onto the preheated baking sheet and bake in the oven for 10-15 minutes, until pale golden and browned in spots. Transfer the flatbread to a rack to cool. Repeat with the remaining two pieces of dough. When cool, break into pieces and serve with dips or cheese. **MAKES 3 FLATBREADS**

BILTONG AND SPRING ONION SODA BREAD

750 ml flour

15 ml castor sugar

5 ml bicarbonate of soda

5 ml salt

60 g pkt grated biltong

1 bunch spring onions (white part only), finely chopped

1 clove garlic, crushed

500 ml buttermilk

Sift the flour, sugar, bicarbonate of soda and salt into a mixing bowl. Stir in the biltong, spring onions and garlic and mix well. Add enough buttermilk to form a soft but not sticky dough. Turn the dough onto a floured surface and knead lightly. Shape into a round and place onto a greased baking tray. Pat the dough out a little and cut a deep cross in the centre. Bake in a preheated oven at 200 °C for 30-40 minutes. Insert a skewer into the loaf to test if it is done. If cooked, the skewer comes out clean. **MAKES 1 LOAF**

Rustic rosemary flatbread

BREADS

A TRIO OF BREADS USING ONE BASIC DOUGH

BASIC BREAD DOUGH

4 x 250 ml flour   15 ml sugar

5 ml salt   45 ml olive oil

10 g instant yeast   300–400 ml lukewarm water

Combine the flour, salt, yeast and sugar in a bowl. Add the oil and enough water to form a dough that is soft but not sticky. Knead well until the dough is smooth and elastic. This can be done with the help of a dough hook in an electric mixer or by hand. Place the dough into an oiled plastic bag or bowl and leave to rise until double in size. Remove the dough from the bag or bowl and place on a lightly floured surface. Knead lightly and shape as required.

rosemary fougasse

1 quantity basic dough, 30 ml olive oil, 45 ml chopped fresh rosemary, sea salt flakes for sprinkling

Divide the dough into two portions. Roll out each portion into a rectangle about 20 x 30 cm in size. Place each rectangle onto a greased baking tray and cut slits diagonally down each side of the dough. Open the slits out with your fingers. Cover with a cloth and leave to rise for about 20 minutes. Brush with the olive oil and sprinkle with the rosemary and salt. Bake in a preheated oven at 200 °C for 20–30 minutes, until golden brown. Remove the loaves from the oven and place on a rack to cool. **MAKES 2 LOAVES**

olive oil focaccia

1 quantity basic dough, 80 ml olive oil, 2 cloves garlic, crushed, 1 strip lemon peel, few sprigs thyme,
   sea salt flakes for sprinkling

Combine the olive oil, garlic, lemon peel and thyme in a bowl. Leave to infuse for about 20 minutes. Roll out the dough to fit a 30 x 40 cm greased oven tray. Cover with a cloth and leave to rise for about 20 minutes. Using the handle of a wooden spoon, make indentations all over the dough. Remove the strip of lemon peel from the oil and pour the oil over the dough. Sprinkle with salt. Bake in a preheated oven at 200 °C for 30–40 minutes, until golden brown. Remove from the oven and cool on a rack. **MAKES 1 LARGE LOAF**

deep-pan pizza bread

1 quantity basic dough, 180 ml ready-made tomato pasta sauce, 375 ml grated cheddar cheese,
   375 ml grated mozzarella cheese, toppings of your choice, such as mushrooms, olives, salami,
   ham or pineapple

Divide the dough into two portions. Roll each out to fit a 20 x 30 cm greased oven tray. Spread the tomato sauce over each, sprinkle with a mixture of both cheeses and top with toppings of your choice. Bake in a preheated oven at 200 °C for 20–25 minutes, until the base is golden brown and the topping is cooked. Remove from the oven and allow to cool slightly before removing from the trays. Cut into squares and serve. **MAKES 2 LARGE PIZZAS**

Olive oil focaccia

WHOLEWHEAT BUTTERMILK ROLLS

500 ml Nutty Wheat flour

500 ml cake flour

10 ml salt

10 g instant yeast

25 ml sugar

400–500 ml buttermilk, warmed

60 g butter, melted

1 egg

200–300 ml warm water

1 egg, beaten for glazing

Combine both kinds of flour with the salt, yeast and sugar in a large mixing bowl. In a separate bowl, combine the buttermilk, butter and egg and mix. Add to the dry ingredients with sufficient warm water to form a dough that is soft but not sticky. Knead well until the dough is smooth and elastic. Place the dough in an oiled plastic bag and leave in a warm place to rise until double in size. Remove from the bag, knead lightly and divide into 18 balls. Place the balls, spaced slightly apart, into a greased 30 cm springform tin. Cover the tin with plastic wrap and leave the dough to rise for 20 minutes. Brush each ball with the beaten egg and bake in a preheated oven at 200 °C for 20–30 minutes, until golden brown. Remove the rolls from the tin and serve warm. **MAKES 18 ROLLS**

FLOURLESS CORN BREAD

6 x 250 ml frozen corn

60–80 ml water

12.5 ml salt

15 ml sugar

3 extra-large eggs

60 g butter

Place the corn in a microwavable dish and sprinkle the water over. Cover with vented cling film and microwave on high for 6–8 minutes until tender. Drain well. Place the corn in a food processor and process until it resembles a coarse mass. Add the salt, sugar, eggs and butter and process until mixed through. Spray a medium loaf pan with non-stick cooking spray and line the base with greaseproof paper. Pour the mixture into the pan and bake in a preheated oven at 180 °C for 60–75 minutes. Serve warm or at room temperature. **MAKES 1 LOAF**

MEDITERRANEAN CROWN BREAD

830 ml flour

10 ml salt

10 g instant yeast

10 ml sugar

300 ml hot water

200 ml plain yoghurt or buttermilk

30 g butter, melted

250 ml grated mozzarella cheese

180 ml grated cheddar cheese

60 ml grated Parmesan cheese

125 g small cherry tomatoes, each sliced into 3-4 slices

handful fresh basil, chopped

freshly ground black pepper

Combine the flour, salt, yeast and sugar in a large bowl. In a jug, combine the water and yoghurt or buttermilk and stir. Add enough of the liquid to the flour mixture to make a soft dough. It is better for the dough to be a little too wet than too dry. Place the dough on a lightly floured surface and knead for 5 minutes until smooth and elastic. Place in a large oiled plastic bag and leave in a warm place to double in size - approximately 45 minutes.

Knock back the dough by kneading gently. Roll into a rectangle approximately 25 x 35 cm in size. Using a pastry brush, spread the melted butter over the dough. Sprinkle with the cheeses, top with the cherry tomatoes and basil, and season with black pepper. Roll up from the long side, like a Swiss roll. Using scissors, cut lengthways right through the dough, but not quite to the end. You will end up with two long pieces joined at one end. Carefully plait these two pieces together and then twist into a circle shape, pressing the ends together to form a closed ring. Place on a lightly greased baking tray. Grease a small ovenproof bowl and place in the centre of the bread so that it keeps its round shape. Cover with a cloth and leave to rise for 15 minutes. Bake in a preheated oven at 220 °C for 15 minutes. Reduce the heat to 200 °C and bake for a further 15-20 minutes, until well risen and golden brown. This bread is best enjoyed warm. **MAKES 1 LARGE LOAF**

SEEDED BEER BREAD

4 x 250 ml cake flour	50 g feta cheese, crumbled
15 ml baking powder	45 ml mixed toasted seeds (sunflower,
10 ml salt	pumpkin, sesame)
5 ml dry mustard powder	150 ml buttermilk
45 ml chopped chives	1 extra-large egg
500 ml grated cheddar cheese	340 ml beer

Sift the flour, baking powder, salt and mustard powder into a large mixing bowl. Stir in the chives, cheeses and seeds. In a separate bowl, combine the buttermilk and egg. Add this to the dry ingredients along with the beer. Mix well to form a stiff batter. Spoon the mixture into a 13 x 23 cm loaf pan sprayed with non-stick cooking spray. Bake in a preheated oven at 180 °C for 50–60 minutes, or until a skewer comes out clean when inserted into the middle. Cool in the pan for about 5 minutes before transferring to a cooling rack. **MAKES 1 LOAF**

RYE BREAD

500 ml rye flour	15 ml brown sugar
500 ml cake flour	10 g instant yeast
10 ml salt	30 ml treacle or molasses or honey
30 g butter	300–400 ml lukewarm water

Combine the rye flour, cake flour and salt in a mixing bowl. Rub in the butter with fingertips until the mixture resembles breadcrumbs. Stir in the sugar and yeast. In a jug, dissolve the treacle in the water. Add enough of the treacle liquid to the mixture to make a soft but not sticky dough. Turn the dough out onto a lightly floured surface and knead well for about 5 minutes until smooth and elastic. Place the dough in a large lightly oiled plastic bag and leave in a warm place for about 40 minutes until the dough has doubled in size. Remove the dough from the bag and knead lightly on a floured surface. Divide in half and shape each half into an oval-shaped loaf. Place on a large baking tray sprayed with non-stick cooking spray. Lightly slash the top of each loaf diagonally three times with a very sharp knife and sift over a little extra rye flour. Cover with a cloth and leave to rise for 20 minutes. Bake in a preheated oven at 200 °C for 15 minutes, then reduce the temperature to 180 °C and bake for a further 15–20 minutes, until the loaves sound hollow when tapped underneath. **MAKES 2 LOAVES**

Seeded beer bread

HEALTH BREAD

500 ml wholewheat flour	250 ml cranberries
500 ml cake flour	20 ml bicarbonate of soda
250 ml digestive bran	3 ml salt
100 g pecan nuts, chopped	500 ml buttermilk
250 ml mixed seeds (sesame, poppy, sunflower, linseed)	125 ml honey

Combine all the dry ingredients in a large bowl and mix well. Make a well in the centre and stir in the buttermilk and honey. Mix well. Spoon the mixture into a 30 x 12 cm loaf pan sprayed with non-stick cooking spray. Bake in a preheated oven at 180 °C for 50-60 minutes or until a skewer comes out clean when inserted into the middle. If the loaf begins to brown too quickly on top, cover with foil and lower the oven temperature to 160 °C until cooked through. Remove from the pan and cool on a cooling rack.
MAKES 1 LOAF

POTATO AND ONION WEDGES

500 ml flour	50 g Parmesan cheese, grated
20 ml baking powder	60 ml chopped chives
100 g butter	80-100 ml milk
15 ml olive oil	1 egg, beaten for glazing
1 onion, finely chopped	15 ml poppy seeds
2 medium potatoes, peeled, cooked and mashed	

Sift the flour and baking powder into a large mixing bowl. Rub in the butter until the mixture resembles coarse breadcrumbs. Heat the oil in a small frying pan and cook the onion until soft but not discoloured. Allow the onion to cool before stirring into the flour mixture. Add the mashed potatoes, cheese and chives. Stir in enough milk to form a dough that is soft but not sticky. Turn onto a floured surface and knead lightly. Shape into a 20 cm round about 2 cm thick and place on a baking sheet sprayed with non-stick cooking spray. Score into eight wedges. Brush the top with the beaten egg, sprinkle with the poppy seeds and bake in a preheated oven at 190 °C for 30-40 minutes. Remove from the oven and cool. Serve with lashings of butter. **MAKES 8 WEDGES**

Health bread

MUFFINS
AND SCONES

APPLE STREUSEL MUFFINS

These muffins are incredibly moist and have a tasty, crunchy topping.

500 ml cake flour

15 ml baking powder

5 ml ground cinnamon

pinch of salt

125 ml white sugar

1 extra-large egg

125 ml milk

125 ml buttermilk

80 g butter, melted

1 Granny Smith apple, cored and coarsely chopped (do not peel)

60 ml raisins

STREUSEL TOPPING

80 ml soft brown sugar

7.5 ml ground cinnamon

50 g pecan nuts, chopped

For the muffins, sift the flour, baking powder, cinnamon and salt into a large mixing bowl. Stir in the sugar. In a measuring jug, combine the egg, milk, buttermilk and melted butter, then mix this into the dry ingredients until just combined. Stir in the apple and raisins.

For the topping, combine all the ingredients.

Spray a muffin pan with non-stick cooking spray and half-fill with the muffin batter. Sprinkle half the streusel mixture on top, then top with the remaining batter. Sprinkle the remaining streusel topping over each muffin. Bake in a preheated oven at 180 °C for 20–25 minutes. **MAKES 12 STANDARD**

Apple streusel muffins

CHOCOLATE MUFFINS

250 ml cake flour	CHOCOLATE GLACÉ ICING
pinch of salt	250 ml icing sugar
10 ml baking powder	25 ml cocoa powder
45 ml cocoa powder	boiling water to mix
125 ml white sugar	
1 extra-large egg	
80 ml sunflower oil	
160 ml milk	

For the muffins, sift the flour, salt, baking powder and cocoa powder into a large bowl. Add the sugar. In a separate bowl, combine the egg, oil and milk, then stir this mixture into the dry ingredients until just combined. Spoon the mixture into muffin pans sprayed with non-stick cooking spray and bake in a preheated oven at 200 °C for 20 minutes. Remove from the oven and place on a cooling rack.

For the icing, sift the icing sugar and cocoa powder together and mix with enough boiling water to make a runny icing. Ice the muffins once they have cooled completely. **MAKES 8–10 STANDARD**

BEST BANANA MUFFINS

This is an economical recipe that produces really moist muffins with a good keeping quality.

4 ripe bananas, mashed
200 ml white sugar
1 extra-large egg
80 g butter, melted
375 ml cake flour
5 ml baking powder
5 ml bicarbonate of soda
pinch of salt

Combine the bananas, sugar and egg in a large mixing bowl. Stir in the melted butter. In a separate bowl, sift the remaining ingredients together, then add this to the banana mixture. Mix lightly until just combined.

Spoon the mixture into muffin pans sprayed with non-stick cooking spray and bake in a preheated oven at 180 °C for about 20 minutes. Leave to cool for 5 minutes, then remove from the pan and cool on a cooling rack. **MAKES 12 STANDARD**

Chocolate muffins

MUFFINS AND SCONES

SAVOURY LIME MUFFINS

Serve these muffins halved and topped with cream cheese and smoked salmon. When made into mini muffins, they are the perfect mouthful for a cocktail party.

375 ml self-raising flour, sifted
15 ml white sugar
20 ml grated lime rind
60 ml olive oil
250 ml plain yoghurt
2 extra-large eggs
milk (if necessary)

Place the flour, sugar and lime rind into a mixing bowl. In a separate bowl, combine the oil, yoghurt and eggs and mix well. Add this to the dry ingredients and mix to combine. The mixture should be of a stiff dropping consistency; add a little milk if necessary.

Spoon into muffin pans sprayed with non-stick cooking spray. Bake in a preheated oven at 180 °C for 20 minutes for standard and 15 minutes for mini muffins. Remove and cool. **MAKES 10–12 STANDARD OR 18 MINI**

STICKY LIME AND POPPY SEED MUFFINS

All the rage! The lime gives these muffins a special flavour.

500 ml cake flour	1 extra-large egg
15 ml baking powder	100 ml sunflower oil
45 ml poppy seeds	
180 ml white sugar	SYRUP
grated rind of 2 limes	juice of 2 limes
125 ml plain yoghurt	125 ml white sugar
125 ml milk	

For the muffins, sift the flour and baking powder into a large bowl. Stir in the poppy seeds, sugar and lime rind. In a separate bowl, combine the yoghurt, milk, egg and oil and whisk together lightly. Add this to the dry ingredients, stirring until just combined.

Spoon the batter into muffin pans sprayed with non-stick cooking spray and bake in a preheated oven at 180 °C for 20 minutes.

For the syrup, prepare by heating the lime juice and sugar together in a pan, stirring until the sugar has dissolved. Remove the muffins from the oven and pour a little of the hot syrup over each while still hot in the pan. **MAKES 12 STANDARD**

Savoury lime muffins

HEALTH MUFFINS

An excellent idea for breakfast on the run, and great for lunchboxes too.

250 ml cake flour	250 ml grated carrots
250 ml wholewheat flour	grated rind and juice of 1 orange
125 ml digestive bran	60 ml honey
20 ml baking powder	80 ml sunflower oil
pinch of salt	2 extra-large eggs
50 g pecan nuts, chopped	250 ml plain yoghurt
125 g dates, pitted and chopped	

Combine the cake and wholewheat flours, bran, baking powder, salt, nuts, dates, carrots and grated orange rind in a large bowl and mix together well. Place the orange juice, honey, oil, eggs and yoghurt in a measuring jug and mix together lightly. Pour this into the dry ingredients and mix until just combined.

Spoon the mixture into muffin pans sprayed with non-stick cooking spray and bake in a preheated oven at 180 °C for 20–25 minutes. Remove the muffins from the pan and place on a cooling rack to cool completely. **MAKES 10–12 STANDARD**

COFFEE-PECAN MUFFINS

500 ml cake flour

125 ml light brown sugar

15 ml baking powder

100 g butter, cut into cubes

100 g pecan nuts, chopped

20 ml instant coffee powder dissolved in 30 ml hot water

250 ml buttermilk

1 extra-large egg

icing sugar, sifted for dusting

Sift the flour, sugar and baking powder together into a bowl. Rub in the butter and stir in the nuts. In a separate bowl, combine the dissolved coffee, buttermilk and egg, then add this to the dry ingredients and mix until just combined.

Spoon into muffin pans sprayed with non-stick cooking spray and bake in a preheated oven at 200 °C for about 20 minutes. Remove and place on a cooling rack. When cool, dust lightly with sifted icing sugar. **MAKES 10–12 STANDARD**

HONEY AND YOGHURT MUFFINS

The combination of oats, yoghurt and honey with a touch of spice is almost a breakfast-in-one muffin.

500 ml cake flour

5 ml bicarbonate of soda

10 ml baking powder

60 ml light brown sugar

5 ml ground mixed spice

125 ml oats

60 g butter, melted

175 ml plain yoghurt

80 ml milk

1 extra-large egg

60 ml runny honey

Sift the flour, bicarbonate of soda, baking powder, sugar and spice into a mixing bowl. Stir in the oats. In a separate bowl, combine the melted butter, yoghurt, milk, egg and honey, then add this to the dry ingredients and mix until just combined.

Spoon into muffin pans sprayed with non-stick cooking spray and bake in a preheated oven at 200 °C for about 20 minutes. Remove and place on a cooling rack. **MAKES 10–12 STANDARD**

GRANADILLA AND MINT MUFFINS

In these muffins, the addition of fresh mint brings out the flavour of the granadilla.

500 ml cake flour	buttermilk
125 ml castor sugar	1 extra-large egg
15 ml baking powder	
100 g butter, cut into cubes	ICING
125 ml finely chopped fresh mint	60 ml icing sugar
1 x 170 g can granadilla pulp	15 ml lemon juice

For the muffins, sift the flour, castor sugar and baking powder into a mixing bowl. Rub in the butter, then add the mint. Pour the granadilla pulp into a measuring jug and add just enough buttermilk to make up 250 ml. Beat in the egg, then add this mixture to the dry ingredients and mix until just combined.

Spoon into muffin pans sprayed with non-stick cooking spray. Bake in a preheated oven at 200 °C for 20 minutes. Remove the muffins from the pan and place on a cooling rack.

For the icing, combine the icing sugar and lemon juice to form a thick glacé icing. Spoon the icing over while the muffins are still warm or drizzle over when cool. **MAKES 10–12 STANDARD**

MUFFINS AND SCONES

CRANBERRY AND WHITE CHOCOLATE MUFFINS

Dried cranberries have become more readily available from speciality food stores and add a unique flavour to baking. This is a decadent recipe.

500 ml cake flour

10 ml baking powder

2.5 ml bicarbonate of soda

125 ml white sugar

grated rind of 1 lemon

100 g white cooking chocolate, roughly chopped

100 g dried cranberries

1 extra-large egg

80 ml sunflower oil

250 ml plain yoghurt

milk to mix (if necessary)

extra white chocolate, melted, for decoration (optional)

Sift the flour, baking powder, bicarbonate of soda and sugar together into a mixing bowl. Add the lemon rind, chocolate and cranberries. In a separate bowl, combine the egg, oil and yoghurt and mix well. Add this to the dry ingredients and mix until just combined, adding a little milk if necessary; the batter should be of a stiff dropping consistency.

Spoon into muffin pans sprayed with non-stick cooking spray and bake in a preheated oven at 200 °C for 20 minutes. Remove the muffins from the oven and place on a cooling rack. When cooled, drizzle with extra melted chocolate if desired. **MAKES 10–12 STANDARD**

Cranberry and white chocolate muffins

CARAMELIZED ONION AND POPPY SEED MUFFINS

Red onions are so much sweeter than ordinary white ones, but can be easily replaced with these if the red ones are unavailable.

75 ml olive oil

2 red onions, halved and thinly sliced

15 ml treacle brown sugar

45 ml chopped fresh sage or 10 ml dried

500 ml cake flour

15 ml baking powder

5 ml mustard powder

5 ml salt

freshly ground black pepper to taste

30 ml poppy seeds

250 ml grated cheddar cheese

1 extra-large egg, lightly beaten

about 300 ml milk

Heat 30 ml of the olive oil in a small saucepan and gently fry the onions over low heat for 10–15 minutes. Stir in the sugar and sage, cook a few minutes, then remove from the heat and set aside to cool. Sift the flour, baking powder and mustard powder into a large bowl and season with salt and pepper. Stir in the poppy seeds, cheese and cooled onion mixture. Add the egg and remaining olive oil and just enough milk to form a soft dough. Do not overmix.

Spoon the mixture into muffin pans sprayed with non-stick cooking spray and bake in a preheated oven at 180 °C for 20–25 minutes. Cool on a cooling rack. **MAKES 10–12 STANDARD**

Caramelized onion and poppy seed muffins

PEAR AND BLUE CHEESE MUFFINS

Pear and blue cheese are a perfect combination.

500 ml cake flour

15 ml baking powder

5 ml salt

100 g blue cheese, crumbled

250 ml grated cheddar cheese

1 bunch spring onions (white part only), finely chopped

60 ml chopped fresh parsley

2 ripe pears, cored, peeled and chopped

80 ml sunflower oil

250 ml milk

1 extra-large egg

Sift the flour, baking powder and salt into a mixing bowl. Add both cheeses, the spring onions, parsley and pears. Mix well. In a separate bowl, combine the oil, milk and egg and mix well. Add this to the dry ingredients and mix gently until well blended.

Spoon into muffin pans sprayed with non-stick cooking spray and bake in a preheated oven at 200 °C for about 20 minutes. Remove and place on a cooling rack. **MAKES 10–12 STANDARD**

CHEESE AND BACON MUFFINS

500 ml cake flour

15 ml baking powder

5 ml salt

10 ml mustard powder

500 ml grated mature cheddar cheese

125 g bacon, fried and finely chopped

60 ml chopped fresh parsley

250 ml buttermilk

100 ml sunflower oil

1 extra-large egg

Sift the flour, baking powder, salt and mustard powder into a mixing bowl and mix well. Add the cheese, bacon and parsley and mix. In a separate bowl, combine the buttermilk, oil and egg, then add this to the dry ingredients and mix until just combined.

Spoon into muffin pans sprayed with non-stick cooking spray and bake in a preheated oven at 200 °C for about 20 minutes. Remove and place on a cooling rack. **MAKES 10–12 STANDARD**

Pear and blue cheese muffins

OLIVE AND PESTO MUFFINS

500 ml cake flour

15 ml baking powder

5 ml salt

375 ml grated mature cheddar cheese

1 bunch spring onions (white part only), chopped

100 g olives, pitted and chopped

200 ml buttermilk

50 ml ready-made pesto (any flavour)

80 ml sunflower oil

1 extra-large egg

Sift the flour, baking powder and salt into a mixing bowl. Add the cheese, spring onions and olives and mix well. In a separate bowl, combine the buttermilk, pesto, oil and egg and mix well. Add this to the dry ingredients and mix until just combined.

Spoon into muffin pans sprayed with non-stick cooking spray and bake in a preheated oven at 200 °C for about 20 minutes for standard and 15 minutes for mini muffins. Remove and place on a cooling rack.
MAKES 10–12 STANDARD OR 18 MINI

CHILLI-CORN MUFFINS

500 ml cake flour

15 ml baking powder

125 ml polenta

5 ml salt

500 ml grated cheddar cheese

1 x 410 g can whole kernel corn, well drained

125 ml chopped fresh coriander

1–2 fresh red chillies, seeded and finely chopped

250 ml buttermilk

100 ml sunflower oil

1 extra-large egg

Sift the flour, baking powder, polenta and salt into a mixing bowl. Add the cheese, corn, coriander and chillies. Mix well. In a separate bowl, combine the buttermilk, oil and egg, then mix this into the dry ingredients until just combined.

Spoon into muffin pans sprayed with non-stick cooking spray and bake in a preheated oven at 200 °C for about 20 minutes. Remove and place on a cooling rack. MAKES 10–12 STANDARD

Olive and pesto muffins

MUFFINS AND SCONES

BUTTERMILK SCONES

Serve these scones with strawberry jam and whipped cream.

4 x 250 ml cake flour
pinch of salt
30 ml baking powder
120 g butter, cut into cubes
80 ml white sugar
250 ml buttermilk
1 extra-large egg
60–80 ml water
extra beaten egg for glazing

Sift the flour, salt and baking powder into a large bowl. Lightly rub the butter into the flour mixture using fingertips, until the mixture resembles coarse breadcrumbs. Stir in the sugar. In a separate bowl, combine the buttermilk and egg and, using a round-bladed knife, stir this into the flour mixture with enough water to make a soft but not sticky dough. The dough should come together and leave the sides of the bowl clean.

Turn the dough onto a floured surface and knead lightly until the mixture forms a ball. Using lightly floured fingers, pat the dough to 3 cm thick. Cut out the scones using a 7 cm diameter scone cutter and place on a baking sheet sprayed with non-stick cooking spray. Gather up the trimmings, lightly knead together again and cut out the last scone. Brush each scone with a little beaten egg and bake in a preheated oven at 220 °C for 12–15 minutes. The cooked scones should sound hollow when tapped underneath. Cool on a cooling rack. **MAKES 10-12**

VARIATION
wholewheat scones
Replace 500 ml of the cake flour with 500 ml wholewheat flour and reduce the sugar to 50 ml.

Buttermilk scones

MUFFINS AND SCONES

CHEESE SCONES

Best eaten on the day, serve these scones split, buttered and topped with grated cheese.

500 ml cake flour

pinch of salt

15 ml baking powder

30 ml white sugar

375 ml grated cheddar cheese

1 extra-large egg

80 ml sunflower oil

125 ml milk

Sift the flour, salt and baking powder into a large bowl. Stir in the sugar and cheese. In a separate bowl, lightly beat the egg, oil and milk together and, using a round-bladed knife, stir this into the dry ingredients to make a soft dough. Press out the dough to 2 cm thick on a lightly floured surface and cut out the scones using a round, 6 cm diameter cutter. Place the scones on a baking sheet sprayed with non-stick cooking spray and bake at 220 °C for about 15 minutes. Remove and cool on a cooling rack. **MAKES 8-10**

SUGAR-CRUSTED ORANGE AND ROSEMARY SCONES

The combination of orange and rosemary gives these great brunch scones a wonderful flavour.
If preferred, the dough can be cut into individual scones and baked.

500 ml cake flour

15 ml baking powder

30 ml castor sugar

60 g butter, cut into cubes

grated rind of 1 orange

25 ml chopped fresh rosemary

1 extra-large egg

100-125 ml milk

extra milk for glazing

light brown sugar for sprinkling

Sift the flour, baking powder and castor sugar into a mixing bowl. Rub in the butter until the mixture resembles breadcrumbs, then add the rind and rosemary. In a separate bowl, combine the egg and milk, then add this to the dry ingredients and mix to form a dough that is soft but not sticky. Turn onto a floured surface and knead gently. Press the dough into a round (20-25 cm diameter) about 2 cm thick and use a knife to score into eight wedges. Place onto a baking sheet sprayed with non-stick cooking spray. Brush the scones with milk and sprinkle with brown sugar. Bake in a preheated oven at 200 °C for 15-20 minutes. Remove and cool. **MAKES 8**

MUFFINS AND SCONES

SPINACH AND FETA SCONES

These scones are best eaten on the day.

750 ml cake flour

25 ml baking powder

5 ml salt

freshly ground black pepper

15 ml white sugar

50 g butter, cut into cubes

200 g feta cheese, crumbled

125 ml grated cheddar cheese

200 g spinach, cooked, well drained and chopped

80 ml peppadews, well drained and chopped

1 extra-large egg

125 ml buttermilk

about 60 ml water

extra beaten egg for glazing

Sift the flour, baking powder, salt, pepper and sugar into a large bowl. Rub in the butter until the mixture resembles breadcrumbs. Stir in both cheeses, the spinach and peppadews. In a separate bowl, combine the egg and buttermilk, then stir this into the dry ingredients, adding just enough water to make a soft but not sticky dough. Sprinkle a little flour onto the work surface and pat the dough out to 2.5 cm thick. Using a 5 cm diameter scone cutter, cut into rounds. Place the scones on a baking sheet sprayed with non-stick cooking spray and brush each one with a little beaten egg to glaze. Bake in a preheated oven at 220 °C for 12–15 minutes. **MAKES 10-12**

MUFFINS AND SCONES

OLIVE AND ROSEMARY SCONES

These are wonderful savoury scones. Replace the black olives with stuffed or plain green olives if preferred.

500 ml cake flour

5 ml salt

15 ml baking powder

80 g butter, cut into cubes

100 g black olives, pitted and chopped

45 ml chopped fresh rosemary

125 ml grated Parmesan cheese

125 ml buttermilk

1 extra-large egg

extra beaten egg for glazing

coarse salt

Sift the flour, salt and baking powder into a mixing bowl. Rub in the butter until the mixture resembles breadcrumbs. Add the olives, rosemary and Parmesan and mix well. In a separate bowl, combine the buttermilk and egg, then add this to the dry ingredients and mix to form a dough that is soft but not sticky. Turn onto a floured surface and knead gently. Roll out to 2 cm thick and cut out with a round, 6 cm diameter cutter. Place onto a baking sheet sprayed with non-stick cooking spray and brush the scones with beaten egg. Sprinkle with coarse salt and bake in a preheated oven at 200 °C for about 20 minutes. **MAKES 8-10**

Olive and rosemary scones

MUFFINS AND SCONES

EASY CHEESE AND HERB CROISSANTS

This croissant recipe doesn't require hours of labour. The croissants are quick to make and the addition of mature cheddar makes all the difference. Serve warm with lots of butter.

750 ml cake flour

pinch of salt

25 ml baking powder

50 g butter, cut into cubes

500 ml coarsely grated mature cheddar cheese

60 ml finely chopped fresh parsley

10 ml chopped fresh origanum

10 ml chopped fresh thyme

10 ml chopped fresh rosemary

1 extra-large egg

180 ml buttermilk

60 ml water

extra beaten egg for glazing

Sift the flour, salt and baking powder into a large bowl. Rub in the butter until the mixture resembles coarse breadcrumbs. Stir in the cheese and all the herbs. In a separate bowl, combine the egg, buttermilk and water, then stir this into the dry ingredients. Mix until a soft dough is formed.

Divide the dough in half and roll one half into a round, 26 cm in diameter. Cut the round into 8 triangles (wedges). Starting at the wide side of each triangle, roll up the dough to form a crescent shape. Repeat the process with the remaining dough. Place on a baking sheet sprayed with non-stick cooking spray and brush with egg glaze. Bake in a preheated oven at 200 °C for 20 minutes or until the croissants are golden brown. **MAKES 16**

Easy cheese and herb croissants

MUFFINS AND SCONES

STICKY CINNAMON BUNS

CINNAMON FILLING
80 g butter, softened
160 ml treacle brown sugar
20 ml ground cinnamon

DOUGH
500 ml cake flour
5 ml salt
15 ml baking powder
60 g butter, cut into cubes
30 ml white sugar
1 extra-large egg
180 ml milk

GLAZE
125 ml icing sugar
water to make a runny icing

For the filling, combine the softened butter, sugar and cinnamon in a bowl. Beat with a wooden spoon until well mixed. Spread 5 ml of the mixture on the base and around the sides of 12 cups in a standard-size muffin pan sprayed with non-stick cooking spray. Set aside the remaining sugar mixture.

For the dough, sift the flour, salt and baking powder into a bowl. Using your fingertips, rub in the butter until the mixture resembles breadcrumbs. Add the sugar. In a separate bowl, beat the egg and milk together. Make a well in the centre of the flour and pour in the milk mixture. Using a round-bladed knife, stir until the mixture forms a dough. Knead the dough lightly on a floured work surface. Roll the dough out to a 30 x 20 cm rectangle. (Sprinkle extra flour on the work surface and rolling pin if the dough sticks.) Spread the surface of the dough generously with the reserved cinnamon-sugar filling. Roll up the dough, from the long side, to form a sausage shape. Cut into 12 slices. Place the buns, cut side down, in the muffin pans. Bake in a preheated oven at 180 °C for 15–20 minutes. Remove the buns from the oven and cool in the pan for a few minutes. Carefully transfer the buns to a cooling rack.

For the glaze, sift the icing sugar into a small bowl and stir in enough water to make a runny icing. When the buns are cool, drizzle glaze over each one. **MAKES 12**

Sticky cinnamon buns

CAKES

BASIC SPONGE CAKE WITH VARIATIONS

*This is a wonderful cake because it is so versatile. Double or treble the ingredients and batch bake using
one recipe for a variety of bakes. The cakes will also freeze well. This mixture will also make one large
Madeira-style loaf using a 29 x 11 cm loaf pan; change the baking time to 40-50 minutes.*

125 g butter, softened
250 ml white sugar
3 extra-large eggs
500 ml cake flour
15 ml baking powder
2.5 ml salt
5 ml vanilla essence
100 ml milk
50 ml water
strawberry jam for filling
icing sugar for dusting

Cream the butter and sugar together with an electric mixer until light and fluffy. Add the eggs, one at
a time, beating well after each addition. In a separate bowl, sift together the flour, baking powder and
salt. Add this to the creamed mixture, along with the vanilla essence, milk and water. Mix with a wooden
spoon until smooth. Spoon into a deep 20 cm or 23 cm cake pan sprayed with non-stick cooking spray
and bake in a preheated oven at 180 °C for 45-60 minutes until golden in colour and a skewer comes
out clean when tested. Cool completely on a cooling rack, then split in the middle and fill with strawberry
jam. Dust the top with icing sugar.

VARIATIONS
apple crumble cake
Prepare the batter as described above and spoon it into a 23 cm cake pan. Top the batter with
1 x 400 g can unsweetened pie apple slices. Combine 45 ml light brown sugar with 10 ml ground cinnamon
and sprinkle over the apple slices. Bake at 180 °C for 45-60 minutes. Serve with whipped cream.

caraway seed cake
Prepare the batter as described above and stir in 15 ml caraway seeds just after adding the milk and
water. Spoon the batter into the cake pan and, if desired, scatter the top with more caraway seeds. Bake
as for the basic sponge.

Basic sponge cake

CITRUS-POPPY SEED CAKE

250 g butter, softened

500 ml castor sugar

15 ml finely grated lemon or orange rind

6 extra-large eggs, lightly beaten

500 ml cake flour

10 ml baking powder

250 ml sour cream

45 ml poppy seeds

GLAZE

juice of 2 lemons or oranges

125 ml white sugar

For the cake, cream the butter, castor sugar and citrus rind until light and fluffy. Add the eggs and blend well. Sift the flour and baking powder and fold into the creamed mixture alternately with the sour cream. Stir in the poppy seeds. Mix gently until smooth, then pour into a 20 cm springform pan sprayed with non-stick cooking spray. Bake in a preheated oven at 160 °C for 1 hour or until a skewer comes out clean when tested. After baking, leave the cake in the pan for a few minutes, then pour on the glaze. Leave for a few more minutes then remove from the pan.

For the glaze, combine the fruit juice and sugar in a small saucepan, then bring to a gentle boil over a low heat. Boil for 5 minutes, then use while hot to glaze the cake.

LIME DRIZZLE CAKE

The coconut flakes – available from speciality food stores –
are what make this cake so decorative. Delicious served with cream.

180 g butter, softened

250 ml castor sugar

finely grated rind of 3 limes

6 extra-large eggs, lightly beaten

375 ml cake flour, sifted

10 ml baking powder, sifted

200 g desiccated coconut

25 ml coconut flakes, toasted

LIME SYRUP

300 ml white sugar

juice of 3 limes

125 ml water

For the cake, cream the butter, castor sugar and rind in a large bowl until light and fluffy. Add the eggs, flour, baking powder and desiccated coconut. Beat together for 2 minutes on medium speed with an electric beater until well mixed. Spoon the mixture into the lined base of a 20 cm springform pan sprayed with non-stick cooking spray and bake in a preheated oven at 180 °C for 40–45 minutes or until a skewer comes out clean when tested. Prepare the syrup. Remove the cake from the oven and pour the warm syrup over. Leave to stand for about 5 minutes before removing the cake from the tin and placing it on a cooling rack. Decorate with toasted coconut flakes.

For the syrup, combine the sugar, lime juice and water in a small saucepan and dissolve slowly over a low heat. Bring to the boil, then reduce heat and simmer for 5 minutes.

Citrus-poppy seed cake

BUTTERSCOTCH CAKE

This cake has a great caramel flavour and tastes even better the day after baking.

125 g butter

250 ml treacle brown sugar

5 ml vanilla essence

2 extra-large eggs

20 ml golden syrup

375 ml cake flour

10 ml baking powder

2.5 ml ground cinnamon

200 ml milk

BUTTERSCOTCH ICING

60 g butter

125 ml light brown sugar

50 ml fresh cream

375 ml icing sugar, sifted

For the cake, cream the butter and sugar well. Add the vanilla essence and the eggs, one at a time. Add the syrup. Sift the flour, baking powder and cinnamon together. Add to the creamed mixture with the milk and mix. Spoon the batter into a 20 cm round or square cake pan sprayed with non-stick cooking spray and bake in a preheated oven at 170 °C for 40–50 minutes or until a skewer comes out clean when tested. Turn out onto a cooling rack and cool.

For the icing, combine the butter and brown sugar in a small saucepan and heat until the sugar has dissolved. Remove from the heat and add the cream and icing sugar. Mix until smooth. Spread the warm icing over the cooled cake.

Butterscotch cake

BUTTERMILK-PRUNE CAKE

Buttermilk brings such lightness to the texture of a cake. Omit the prunes for a plain buttermilk cake.

125 g butter	finely grated rind of 1 orange
500 ml castor sugar	250 ml buttermilk
4 extra-large eggs	5 ml vanilla essence
750 ml cake flour	250 ml pitted prunes
3 ml bicarbonate of soda	icing sugar for dusting
pinch of salt	

Cream the butter and castor sugar together until light and creamy. Add the eggs, one at a time, beating after each addition. If the mixture curdles, add a little flour. In a separate bowl, sift the flour, bicarbonate of soda and salt together. Add the orange rind, then add this to the creamed mixture along with the buttermilk and vanilla essence. Using kitchen scissors, snip each prune into 3–4 pieces and add to the cake batter. Mix through. Pour the batter into a bundt (tube) pan sprayed with non-stick cooking spray. Bake in a preheated oven at 170 °C for 50–60 minutes or until a skewer comes out clean when tested. Remove the cake from the pan and leave to cool on a cooling rack. Dust with icing sugar before serving.

RAISIN AND CHEESE BREAKFAST CAKE

*The mature cheddar gives this cake a good flavour. Enjoy a slice for breakfast
on the run or as a great brunch idea.*

110 ml white sugar	125 ml raisins
65 g butter	250 ml grated mature cheddar cheese
1 extra-large egg	extra 15 ml cake flour
500 ml cake flour	extra 50 ml white sugar
15 ml baking powder	5 ml ground cinnamon
2.5 ml salt	extra 30 g butter, melted
175 ml milk	

Cream together the first quantities of sugar and butter. Add the egg. In a separate bowl, sift together the flour, baking powder and salt, then add this to the creamed ingredients, together with the milk. Dust the raisins and the cheese with the extra flour, then fold into the cake mixture. Spray a 20 x 23 cm square pan with non-stick cooking spray. Pour the batter into the pan. Combine the extra sugar and cinnamon and sprinkle over the batter. Drizzle over the melted butter. Bake in a preheated oven at 190 °C for 25–30 minutes or until a skewer comes out clean when tested.

Buttermilk-prune cake

ORANGE MARMALADE SYRUP CAKE

If preferred, use crème fraîche instead of yoghurt. Crème fraîche is a cultured cream with
far less fat than ordinary cream.

125 g butter, softened

250 ml castor sugar

rind of 2 oranges (reserve the juice for the syrup)

3 extra-large eggs

250 ml thick plain yoghurt (or crème fraîche or even buttermilk)

45 ml orange marmalade

375 ml cake flour

2.5 ml bicarbonate of soda

5 ml baking powder

ORANGE SYRUP

reserved juice from the oranges

250 ml white sugar

orange slices to decorate (optional)

For the cake, cream the butter and castor sugar in a large bowl until light in colour. Add the orange rind. Add one egg at a time, beating well after each addition. Fold in the yoghurt and marmalade. In a separate bowl, sift the flour, bicarbonate of soda and baking powder together, then add this to the creamed mixture and mix through. Place in a 20 cm ring pan sprayed with non-stick cooking spray and bake in a preheated oven at 170 °C for 40–50 minutes or until a skewer comes out clean when tested. Remove the cake from the pan and place on a cooling rack.

For the syrup, combine the orange juice and sugar in a small saucepan. Bring to the boil, stirring to ensure the sugar dissolves. Allow to boil for 5 minutes to a syrupy consistency. Place the cake on a serving plate and pour over the warm syrup. Decorate with orange slices if desired.

Orange marmalade syrup cake

ITALIAN OLIVE OIL CAKE

Delicious served with coffee and even better accompanied with cream or doused
with vin santo (an Italian sweet wine), or any other dessert wine.
This cake will keep in an airtight container for a couple of days.

4 extra-large eggs, separated	750 ml cake flour
250 ml castor sugar	10 ml baking powder
5 ml vanilla essence	250 ml milk
250 ml olive oil	icing sugar for dusting

In the bowl of an electric mixer, whisk the egg yolks with the castor sugar and vanilla essence until thick and light in colour. Add the olive oil and whisk until mixed through. Sift the flour and baking powder, add to the creamed mixture and whisk lightly. Add the milk. In a separate bowl, beat the egg whites until stiff, then fold into the cake mixture using a spatula. Spray a 23 cm springform or bundt (tube) pan with non-stick cooking spray and spoon the mixture into the pan. Bake in a preheated oven at 180 °C for 45 minutes or until a skewer comes out clean when tested. Cool and dust with icing sugar.

BEER BOX CHOCOLATE CAKE

Great for a crowd because it can be cut into at least 30 slices. Use the carton beer box measuring
27 x 40 cm. Staple the corners before using as the glue can melt in the oven.

500 ml water	ICING
150 ml sunflower oil	125 g butter
100 ml cocoa powder	500 ml icing sugar, sifted
10 ml vanilla essence	50–80 ml milk
8 extra-large eggs	5 ml vanilla essence
750 ml castor sugar	
875 ml cake flour, sifted	
17.5 ml baking powder, sifted	
pinch of salt, sifted	

For the cake, combine the water, oil, cocoa powder and vanilla essence in a saucepan and bring to the boil, stirring until the mixture is smooth. Pour into a large mixing bowl and leave to cool slightly. Using an electric mixer, beat together the eggs and castor sugar until light and almost white in colour. Add to the cocoa mixture together with the dry ingredients. Pour into a foil-lined (shiny side facing upwards) beer box sprayed with non-stick cooking spray. Bake in a preheated oven at 180 °C for 30–35 minutes or until a skewer comes out clean. Cool completely in the box before transferring to a cooling rack.

For the icing, cream the butter, then add the icing sugar, milk and vanilla essence. Mix until smooth. Spread over the cooled cake.

Italian olive oil cake

HOME INDUSTRY YOGHURT-CHOCOLATE CAKE

This cake originated in a magazine cake competition many years ago and is still so popular.

250 g butter

380 ml white sugar

4 extra-large eggs

5 ml bicarbonate of soda

250 ml plain yoghurt

5 ml baking powder, sifted

500 ml cake flour, sifted

pinch of salt, sifted

5 ml vanilla essence

100 g dark chocolate

60 ml milk

TOPPING

125 g butter

250 ml white sugar

100 ml fresh cream

200 ml desiccated coconut

For the cake, cream the butter and sugar until light and creamy. Add the eggs, one at a time, beating well after each addition. Add a little flour if the mixture looks curdled. Dissolve the bicarbonate of soda in the yoghurt and add to the creamed mixture together with the dry ingredients and vanilla essence. Spray a 23 cm springform pan with non-stick cooking spray. Pour the mixture into the pan. Melt the chocolate and milk together in the microwave on medium for 1–2 minutes, stirring once. Pour the chocolate mixture over the raw cake batter; don't stir it in. Bake in a preheated oven at 180 °C for 40–50 minutes or until a skewer comes out clean when tested. Remove from the oven and cover the cooled cake with the topping.

For the topping, combine the butter, sugar and cream in a saucepan, stirring to combine. Bring to the boil, then remove from the heat and add the coconut. Cover the cake with the topping and place it under a preheated grill for a few minutes, watching carefully, until just lightly browned. Cool in the pan.

SWEET WINE GRAPE CAKE

A cake of the Cape and an excellent way of using seedless grapes in a baked item.

375 ml cake flour

5 ml baking powder

5 ml salt

2.5 ml bicarbonate of soda

185 ml castor sugar

100 g butter, at room temperature

45 ml olive oil

2 extra-large eggs

5 ml vanilla essence

250 ml sweet wine or clear apple juice

grated rind of 2 lemons

375 ml seedless grapes

extra 30 g butter

extra 30 ml castor sugar

Sift together the flour, baking powder, salt and bicarbonate of soda. In a separate bowl, beat the castor sugar with the butter and oil until pale and creamy. Beat in the eggs and add the vanilla essence. Gently beat in the flour mixture alternately with the wine or apple juice until just smooth. Add the rind. Turn into a 23 cm springform pan sprayed with non-stick cooking spray. Smooth the top and sprinkle with the grapes, then bake in a preheated oven at 200 °C for about 20 minutes, or until the top is set. Dot with the extra butter and sprinkle with the extra sugar. Bake for a further 20 minutes or until golden and cooked. Leave to cool in the pan for 20 minutes before removing. Serve at room temperature.

PEAR AND HONEY CAKE

Substitute pears with apples if desired. To save on time, canned pears in natural juice can be used and do not require any cooking (you still need to add the lemon juice and honey).

2 large green pears, peeled, cored and halved	160 ml castor sugar
50 ml lemon juice	3 extra-large eggs
50 ml honey	375 ml cake flour
200 g butter	10 ml baking powder
10 ml grated lemon rind	90 ml milk

Place the pear halves in a saucepan with the lemon juice and honey and simmer over low heat for about 5 minutes until just tender. Remove the pears, reserving the juice, and set aside. Cream together the butter, lemon rind and castor sugar until light and fluffy. Add the eggs, one at a time, beating well after each addition. Sift the flour and baking powder and add alternately with the milk to the creamed mixture. Spoon the batter into a 20 cm springform pan or use a heart-shaped pan sprayed with non-stick cooking spray. Thinly slice the pear halves lengthways and arrange decoratively on top of the uncooked batter. Bake in a preheated oven at 180 °C for 50-60 minutes or until a skewer comes out clean when tested. Remove from the oven and brush with the reserved syrup. Cool and remove from the pan.

BUTTERNUT, BEETROOT OR CARROT CAKE

Vegetable cakes are all the rage. Ring the changes from the usual carrot with butternut or beetroot for a pretty speckled cake.

4 extra-large eggs	CREAM CHEESE ICING
310 ml white sugar	80 g butter
250 ml sunflower oil	125 g thick cream cheese
500 ml cake flour	5 ml vanilla essence
10 ml bicarbonate of soda	500 ml icing sugar, sifted
10 ml ground cinnamon	
5 ml salt	
4 x 250 ml peeled and grated raw butternut or beetroot or carrots	
100 g pecan nuts, chopped (optional)	

For the cake, beat the eggs and sugar until thick and pale. Beat in the oil. Sift the flour, bicarbonate of soda, cinnamon and salt and stir into the egg mixture. Mix in the selected grated vegetable and nuts, if using. Spoon the mixture into a 23 cm ring pan or two loaf tins (22 x 12 cm) sprayed with non-stick cooking spray and bake in a preheated oven at 160 °C for 50-60 minutes or until a skewer comes out clean.

For the icing, cream the butter and cream cheese. Add the vanilla essence and icing sugar to make a thick, fluffy icing. Spread over the cooled cake. Decorate with extra pecan nuts if desired.

Pear and honey cake

LEMON-GLAZED CAKE WITH FRESH BERRIES

This cake looks almost too good too eat. It is obviously best baked in berry season, but fresh sliced nectarines or plums can be used instead.

225 g butter, softened

250 ml castor sugar

4 extra-large eggs

grated rind of 1 lemon

375 ml self-raising flour, sifted

25 g ground almonds

30 ml lemon juice

30 ml milk

2 x 125 g punnets mixed berries (blueberries, blackberries, raspberries)

(use seasonal berries or good-quality frozen berries)

SYRUP

125 ml lemon juice

rind of 1 lemon

150 ml castor sugar

For the cake, cream the butter and castor sugar well. Add the eggs, one at a time, beating after each addition. Mix in 15 ml of the flour if the mixture curdles. Add in the rind, flour, almonds, lemon juice and milk to make a dropping consistency. Spoon the batter into a lined (base and sides) 20 cm square cake pan sprayed with non-stick cooking spray. Smooth the surface and arrange the berries on top. Bake in a preheated oven at 180 °C for 30–40 minutes or until a skewer comes out clean when tested.

For the syrup, combine all the syrup ingredients in a small saucepan and heat gently without boiling. Remove the cake from the oven and pour over the hot syrup. Cool the cake in the pan, then remove and peel away the paper.

Lemon-glazed cake with fresh berries

CAKES

YOGHURT CAKE WITH LEMON SYRUP

A wonderful moist cake with a lemony tang.

200 g butter, softened
250 ml castor sugar
5 extra-large eggs, separated
10 ml grated lemon rind
250 ml plain yoghurt
5 ml vanilla essence
560 ml cake flour
10 ml baking powder
2.5 ml bicarbonate of soda

LEMON SYRUP
250 ml castor sugar
180 ml water
1 cinnamon stick
strip of lemon rind
25 ml lemon juice

For the cake, cream the butter and castor sugar well. Add the egg yolks, one at a time, beating well after each addition. Stir in the lemon rind, yoghurt and vanilla essence. Sift the flour, baking powder and bicarbonate of soda and fold into the creamed mixture. In a separate bowl, beat the egg whites until stiff, then fold into the creamed mixture. Spoon into a deep 22 cm cake pan lined then sprayed with non-stick cooking spray. Bake in a preheated oven at 180 °C for 50–60 minutes or until a skewer comes out clean. After 40 minutes, cover the top with foil to prevent the cake from going too brown. Cool in the pan for 5 minutes before turning out onto a cooling rack.

For the syrup, place all the syrup ingredients in a saucepan and heat over a low heat until the sugar has dissolved. Boil for 5 minutes. Strain and pour the warm syrup over the cooled cake. Serve with whipped cream if desired.

Yoghurt cake with lemon syrup

GINGER CAKE
Better eaten the day after baking.

125 g butter
250 ml light brown sugar
2 extra-large eggs
500 ml cake flour
10 ml baking powder
2.5 ml bicarbonate of soda
10 ml ground ginger
5 ml ground cinnamon
250 ml milk
125 ml chopped preserved ginger

ICING
15–20 ml syrup from preserved ginger
250 ml icing sugar, sifted
extra chopped preserved ginger (optional)

For the cake, cream the butter and sugar well. Add the eggs and beat well. Sift the dry ingredients and add to the creamed mixture alternately with the milk. Lastly mix in the chopped ginger. Spoon the batter into a 20 cm ring pan sprayed with non-stick cooking spray. Bake in a preheated oven at 180 °C for 30–40 minutes or until a skewer comes out clean. Cool in the pan for 10 minutes before turning out.

For the icing, add enough syrup to the icing sugar to make a thick icing. Spread over the cooled cake and decorate with extra preserved ginger if desired.

Ginger cake

SEMOLINA CAKE

4 extra-large eggs, separated

80 ml castor sugar

2.5 ml vanilla essence

5 ml grated orange rind

80 ml orange juice

125 ml semolina

50 g ground almonds

SYRUP

1 lemon

1 orange

375 ml castor sugar

375 ml water

5 ml lemon juice

For the cake, beat the egg yolks, castor sugar and vanilla essence together until thick and fluffy. Stir in the orange rind and juice, semolina and almonds. Cover and leave to stand for 20 minutes. Beat the egg whites until stiff, then fold into the semolina mixture. Pour the batter into a 20 cm cake pan lined then sprayed with non-stick cooking spray and bake in a preheated oven at 180 °C for 30–40 minutes or until a skewer comes out clean when tested.

For the syrup, grate the rind from the lemon and orange and place with the remaining ingredients in a saucepan. Heat gently, stirring until the sugar dissolves. Boil for 5 minutes, then cool slightly. Remove the cake from the oven and pour over the syrup. Cool completely and slice.

GOLDEN CAKE

This cake has a lovely coconut-meringue topping, which keeps the cake moist.

125 g butter
250 ml castor sugar
3 extra-large eggs, separated
5 ml vanilla essence
250 ml cake flour
10 ml baking powder
125 ml milk
250 ml desiccated coconut

Cream the butter and 125 ml castor sugar until light and creamy. Add the egg yolks, one at a time, then add the vanilla essence and beat well. Sift the flour and baking powder together and add to the creamed mixture alternately with the milk. Mix through to incorporate all the ingredients. Spoon the batter into a 20 cm springform pan sprayed with non-stick cooking spray. Whisk the egg whites until soft peaks form (if preferred, add a pinch of salt to speed up the process) and gradually add the remaining castor sugar, beating until you have a meringue-like mixture. Fold in the coconut. Gently spoon the meringue over the uncooked cake batter, then bake in a preheated oven at 160 °C for 50–60 minutes or until a skewer comes out clean when tested. Cool the cake completely in the pan, then loosen with a palette knife and transfer to a serving plate.

CAKES

GRAPEFRUIT CAKE

Grapefruit is an under-utilized fruit, which is really good in a cake. For an orange cake, replace the grapefruit juice and segments with orange juice and segments.

500 ml cake flour
300 ml white sugar
10 ml baking powder
5 extra-large eggs, separated
125 ml milk
100 ml grapefruit juice
100 ml sunflower oil
5 ml vanilla essence
pinch of cream of tartar

CREAM CHEESE ICING
80 g butter
125 g thick cream cheese
5 ml vanilla essence
500 ml icing sugar, sifted
grapefruit segments to decorate

For the cake, sift the flour, sugar and baking powder into a large bowl. In a separate bowl, combine the egg yolks, milk, grapefruit juice, oil and vanilla essence and mix well. Add the dry ingredients to the grapefruit mixture and beat. In another bowl, beat the egg whites and cream of tartar until stiff but not dry, then fold into the grapefruit mixture. Spoon into two deep, 20 cm cake pans lined with baking paper and sprayed with non-stick cooking spray. Bake in a preheated oven at 180 °C for 40–50 minutes or until a skewer comes out clean when tested. Cool in the pan, then remove.

For the icing, cream the butter and cream cheese, then add the vanilla essence and icing sugar to make a thick, fluffy icing. Use half the icing to sandwich the cake together, then use the rest for the top of the cake. Decorate with segments of grapefruit.

Grapefruit cake

CAPE GOOSEBERRY CAKE

1 x 410 g can of gooseberries in syrup
200 g butter
250 ml castor sugar
3 extra-large eggs
500 ml cake flour
10 ml baking powder

CREAM CHEESE ICING
80 g butter
125 g thick cream cheese
5 ml vanilla essence
500 ml icing sugar, sifted
fresh gooseberries to decorate (optional)

For the cake, drain the gooseberries and reserve the syrup. Cream the butter and sugar well. Add the eggs, one at a time, and mix well. Sift the flour and baking powder and add to the creamed mixture alternately with 125 ml of the reserved gooseberry syrup. Fold in the gooseberries. Spoon the batter into a deep 22 cm cake pan lined then sprayed with non-stick cooking spray. Bake in a preheated oven at 180 °C for 40–50 minutes or until a skewer comes out clean when tested. Remove from the oven and pour over any remaining syrup. Cool in the pan, then remove and ice with the cream cheese icing.

For the icing, cream the butter and cream cheese, then add the vanilla essence and icing sugar to make a thick, fluffy icing. Ice the cooled cake. Decorate with fresh gooseberries if desired.

VARIATION
blueberry cake
Use a punnet of fresh blueberries instead of gooseberries and use milk instead of reserved syrup when adding the dry ingredients.

Cape gooseberry cake

LAVENDER SPONGE

Only use fresh lavender leaves, taking care to use the correct quantity,
as too much will make the cake bitter.

250 ml cake flour

80 ml cornflour

125 ml castor sugar

10 ml baking powder

60 ml finely chopped fresh lavender leaves

4 extra-large eggs, separated

60 ml sunflower oil

100 ml milk

extra 60 ml castor sugar

LAVENDER CREAM

250 ml fresh cream

25 ml runny honey

15 ml finely chopped fresh lavender leaves

lavender flowers to decorate

For the cake, sift together the flour, cornflour, castor sugar and baking powder. Mix in the lavender leaves. Make a well in the centre and add the egg yolks, oil and milk. Mix to a smooth batter. Beat the egg whites until stiff, then beat in the extra castor sugar. Fold the egg white mixture into the batter. Spoon into a lined but not greased deep 23 cm cake pan. Bake in a preheated oven at 180 °C for 30–35 minutes or until a skewer comes out clean when tested. Remove from the oven and invert the pan onto a cooling rack without removing the cake. Leave to cool completely.

For the lavender cream, whip the cream and honey until stiff. Mix in the lavender leaves. Split the cake in half and sandwich together with half the cream, then spread the remaining cream on top. Decorate with lavender flowers.

Lavender sponge

COFFEE CAKE WITH PECAN CRUMBLE

80 g butter

100 ml light brown sugar

100 ml white sugar

2 extra-large eggs

25 ml instant coffee granules dissolved in

25 ml boiling water and cooled

500 ml cake flour

5 ml baking powder

5 ml bicarbonate of soda

250 ml buttermilk

icing sugar for dusting

PECAN CRUMBLE

18 Tennis® or tea biscuits, crumbled

50 g pecan nuts

125 ml light brown sugar

7.5 ml ground cinnamon

100 g butter, melted

For the cake, cream the butter and both sugars until light and fluffy. Beat in the eggs and the coffee mixture. Sift the dry ingredients and add to the creamed mixture alternately with the buttermilk. Spray a deep 22 cm springform cake pan with non-stick cooking spray. Spread half the cake batter over the base of the pan. Sprinkle with half the crumble mixture. Spread the remaining cake batter over the crumble, then sprinkle the remaining crumble on top. Bake in a preheated oven at 180 °C for 50–60 minutes or until a skewer comes out clean when tested. Cool completely in the pan, then remove and dust with icing sugar before serving.

For the crumble, combine the biscuits, nuts, brown sugar and ground cinnamon together in a food processor and process until it has a crumbly texture. Add the melted butter and process until mixed.

Coffee cake with pecan crumble

TIRAMISU CAKE

Not quite fuss free, but a popular cake that's just like the dessert.

500 ml cake flour

300 ml white sugar

10 ml baking powder

5 extra-large eggs, separated

125 ml milk

100 ml water

100 ml sunflower oil

5 ml vanilla essence

pinch of cream of tartar

FILLING

250 ml fresh cream

60 ml icing sugar

250 g mascarpone cheese

50 ml coffee liqueur

100 ml strong black coffee

100 g dark chocolate, grated

For the cake, sift the flour, sugar and baking powder into a large bowl. In a separate bowl, combine the egg yolks, milk, water, oil and vanilla essence and mix well. Add the flour mixture to the creamed mixture and beat until blended. Beat the egg whites and cream of tartar together until stiff but not dry. Fold into the batter. Pour the mixture into a deep 23 cm round cake pan lined then sprayed with non-stick cooking spray. Bake in a preheated oven at 180 °C for 40-50 minutes or until a skewer comes out clean when tested. Cool the cake completely.

For the filling, whip the cream and icing sugar together until soft peaks form. Add the mascarpone and whip until thick. Mix in 10 ml of the coffee liqueur. Cut the cake in half horizontally and place the base onto a serving plate. Combine the remaining liqueur with the coffee and brush generously onto the base. Spoon half the filling onto the base and sprinkle with half the grated chocolate. Top with the remaining sponge and brush with the leftover coffee mixture. Top with the remaining filling and finish with a layer of grated chocolate.

Tiramisu cake

CHOCOLATE-CAPPUCCINO CAKE

The combination of chocolate and coffee is divine. Enjoy!

100 g butter

250 ml castor sugar

3 extra-large eggs, separated

5 ml vanilla essence

100 g dark chocolate, melted and cooled

500 ml cake flour

10 ml baking powder

30 ml strong instant coffee granules dissolved in

125 ml boiling water and left to cool

125 ml sour cream

extra 80 ml castor sugar

FUDGE ICING

150 g dark chocolate

50 g butter

30 ml strong instant coffee granules

25 ml hot water

500 ml icing sugar

chocolate flakes to decorate

For the cake, cream the butter and castor sugar well. Beat in the egg yolks, vanilla essence and cooled chocolate. Sift the flour and baking powder and add to the chocolate mixture alternately with the cooled dissolved coffee and sour cream. In a separate bowl, whisk the egg whites until stiff, then gradually beat in the extra castor sugar. Fold into the chocolate mixture. Pour the batter into two 20 cm cake pans lined then sprayed with non-stick cooking spray. Bake in a preheated oven at 180 °C for 25–30 minutes or until a skewer comes out clean when tested. Cool in the pan for 5 minutes before turning out.

For the icing, place the chocolate and butter in a heatproof bowl and melt in the microwave on medium for 2 minutes. Dissolve the coffee in the hot water and cool. Add to the chocolate with enough icing sugar to make a thick, glossy icing. Use half the icing to sandwich the cake layers together, then spread the remaining icing on top. Decorate with chocolate flakes.

Chocolate-cappuccino cake

CHOCOLATE-OIL CAKE

A good basic cake that will never let you down.

60 ml cocoa powder

90 ml hot water

5 ml vanilla essence

250 ml cake flour

125 ml castor sugar

10 ml baking powder

pinch of salt

60 ml sunflower oil

4 extra-large eggs, separated

about 100 ml water

extra 80 ml castor sugar

BUTTER ICING

100 g butter, softened

350 ml icing sugar, sifted

45 ml cocoa powder, sifted

water to mix

For the cake, mix the cocoa powder with the hot water and cool. Add the vanilla essence. Sift the flour, castor sugar, baking powder and salt into a bowl. Make a well in the centre and add the oil, egg yolks and the cocoa mixture. Add enough water to make a smooth batter. In a separate bowl, beat the egg whites until stiff, then gradually beat in the extra castor sugar. Fold this into the chocolate mixture. Spoon the batter into two 20 cm cake pans lined but not greased and bake in a preheated oven at 180 °C for 25–30 minutes or until a skewer comes out clean when tested. Invert the pans onto a cooling rack and leave to cool in the cake pans. When completely cold, run a knife around the edge of the pans and remove the cakes.

For the icing, beat the butter until soft and creamy, then gradually add the icing sugar, cocoa powder and just enough water to make a soft spreading consistency. Sandwich the cakes together with half the icing and spread the remaining icing on top.

Chocolate-oil cake

CHOCOLATE-RED WINE CAKE

This cake is for adults and is an excellent ending to a meal, enjoyed with a cup of strong coffee.

200 g butter, softened

250 ml castor sugar

4 extra-large eggs

60 ml cocoa powder

500 ml cake flour

5 ml baking powder

2.5 ml bicarbonate of soda

125 ml red wine

5 ml vanilla essence

150 g dark chocolate, grated

HOT CHOCOLATE SAUCE

30 g butter

60 ml light brown sugar

15 ml cocoa powder, sifted

125 ml fresh cream

50 g dark chocolate, broken into pieces

For the cake, cream the butter and castor sugar together until light and fluffy. Beat in the eggs, one at a time. Sift the cocoa powder, flour, baking powder and bicarbonate of soda and fold into the creamed mixture. Add the red wine and vanilla essence. Fold in the grated chocolate. Spoon the batter into a 20 cm springform pan sprayed with non-stick cooking spray and bake in a preheated oven at 180 °C for 30–40 minutes or until a skewer comes out clean when tested. Remove from the oven and cool on a cake rack.

For the sauce, melt the butter and sugar in a saucepan. Add the cocoa powder, cream and chocolate and heat very gently, stirring until the chocolate melts. Cut the cooled cake in half and use some of the sauce to ice the middle. Sandwich the two halves together, place the cake on a serving plate and pour the remaining warm chocolate sauce over the top.

Chocolate-red wine cake

CHOCOLATE-BUTTERMILK CAKE

A moist chocolate cake with good flavour, which is better eaten the day after baking.

500 ml cake flour

pinch of salt

5 ml bicarbonate of soda

500 ml white sugar

125 g butter

250 ml water

125 ml sunflower oil

125 ml cocoa powder, sifted

2 extra-large eggs

125 ml buttermilk or plain yoghurt

ICING

60 g butter

30 ml cocoa powder, sifted

45 ml buttermilk or plain yoghurt

5 ml vanilla essence

375 ml icing sugar, sifted

extra cocoa powder for dusting

For the cake, sift together the flour, salt and bicarbonate of soda in a large mixing bowl. Add the sugar. Heat the butter, water, oil and cocoa powder together in a small saucepan. Stir to combine, bring to the boil, then immediately remove from the heat and cool slightly. Pour the liquid into the flour mixture and mix well. Whisk together the eggs and buttermilk, then add to the flour mixture. Spray a 30 x 35 cm square cake pan or large ring pan with non-stick cooking spray. Pour in the cake batter and bake in a preheated oven at 180 °C for 25–30 minutes or until a skewer comes out clean when tested. Remove from the oven and cool in the pan for 5 minutes before turning out on a wire rack.

For the icing, melt the butter in a bowl in the microwave for 1 minute. Remove and stir in the cocoa powder, buttermilk, vanilla essence and icing sugar. Mix until smooth, then spread over the cake. (The beauty of this icing is that even if the cake is not completely cooled, the icing can still be spread over.) Dust with cocoa powder before serving.

Chocolate-buttermilk cake

CAKES

CHOCOLATE-MAYONNAISE CAKE

Yes, it's true, mayonnaise can be used to make a good chocolate cake.
The hazelnuts can be omitted if preferred.

700 ml cake flour

200 ml cocoa powder

375 ml castor sugar

5 ml salt

7.5 ml bicarbonate of soda

300 ml good quality thick mayonnaise (don't use
the low-fat variety)

400 ml water

5 ml vanilla essence

50 g hazelnuts, skinned, toasted and lightly chopped

ICING
100 g slab of dark chocolate, broken into pieces

30 ml fresh cream

15 g butter

30 g hazelnuts, roasted and skinned for decoration

cocoa powder for dusting

For the cake, sift the flour, cocoa powder, castor sugar, salt and bicarbonate of soda together in a mixing bowl. In a separate bowl, combine the mayonnaise, water and vanilla essence and mix through using a balloon whisk. Add this to the flour mixture and mix until smooth. Add the hazelnuts. Pour the batter into a 25 cm ring pan sprayed with non-stick cooking spray. Bake in a preheated oven at 180 °C for 45–50 minutes or until a skewer comes out clean when tested. Turn out onto a cooling rack and cool completely.

For the icing, melt the chocolate, cream and butter together in a bowl over a pan of boiling water, or in the microwave on medium for 2–3 minutes. Allow the mixture to cool and thicken slightly, then pour it over the cooled cake and leave to set. Decorate with the roasted hazelnuts and dust with cocoa powder.

Chocolate-mayonnaise cake

CAKES

CHOCOLATE-CHILLI CAKE

Believe it or not, the chilli brings out the chocolate flavour.

250 g butter

300 ml castor sugar

5 extra-large eggs

400 ml cake flour

10 ml baking powder

180 ml cocoa powder

60 ml milk

5 ml Tabasco sauce

FILLING

60 g butter, softened

250 ml icing sugar, sifted

5 ml dried chilli flakes

grated rind and juice of 1 orange

TOPPING

45 ml golden syrup

juice of 1 orange

100 g dark chocolate

few drops of Tabasco sauce

For the cake, cream the butter and castor sugar together until light and creamy. Add the eggs, one at a time, beating after each addition. Sift the flour, baking powder and cocoa powder together. Add to the creamed mixture alternately with the milk mixed with the Tabasco sauce. Spoon the mixture into two 20 cm cake pans lined with greaseproof paper and sprayed with non-stick cooking spray. Bake in a preheated oven at 180 °C for 25–30 minutes or until a skewer comes out clean when tested. Cool for 10 minutes in the pan before turning out onto a cooling rack.

For the filling, cream the butter and icing sugar together. Add the chilli flakes, orange rind and enough orange juice to make a spreading consistency. Sandwich the cake layers together with the filling.

For the topping, combine all the ingredients in a saucepan and heat over a gentle heat until melted and smooth. Spread the chocolate topping over the cake and decorate as desired.

Chocolate-chilli cake

CHOCOLATE, ORANGE AND PRUNE CAKE

Decadently rich, but really good served in slices with a dollop of fresh cream.

250 g pitted prunes, coarsely chopped

60 ml orange-flavoured liqueur or orange juice or flavoured tea

finely grated rind of 1 orange

60 ml cocoa powder

100 g good quality dark chocolate

50 g butter

200 ml castor sugar

100 ml hot water

3 extra-large eggs, separated

150 ml cake flour, sifted

Combine the prunes, liqueur and orange rind in a bowl and leave to soak for about 30 minutes. Place the cocoa powder, chocolate, butter, 150 ml castor sugar and the hot water in a saucepan and heat gently, stirring until the mixture is smooth. Remove from the heat and cool slightly. Add the egg yolks and stir through. Whisk the egg whites until soft peaks form, then gradually whisk in the remaining castor sugar. Using a metal spoon, gently fold the flour and chocolate mixture into the egg whites. Pour the mixture evenly into a 20 cm springform pan lined then sprayed with non-stick cooking spray. Scatter the prunes and any leftover liqueur over the top of the batter. Bake in a preheated oven at 180 °C for about 30 minutes, until a skewer comes out clean when tested. Leave to cool in the pan for 10 minutes before turning out on a wire rack.

Chocolate, orange and prune cake

CHOCOLATE FUDGE CAKE

125 g butter, softened
375 ml treacle brown sugar
2 extra-large eggs
150 ml sour cream
300 ml cake flour
5 ml baking powder
2.5 ml bicarbonate of soda
125 ml cocoa powder

ICING
50 g butter
40 ml water
60 ml castor sugar
250 ml icing sugar
30 ml cocoa powder
chocolate-dipped pecan nuts to decorate (optional)

For the cake, cream the butter and sugar together until light and creamy. Beat in the eggs, one at a time, then add the sour cream. Sift the flour, baking powder, bicarbonate of soda and cocoa powder together, then fold into the creamed mixture. Spoon the batter into a 20 cm cake pan lined then sprayed with non-stick cooking spray and bake in a preheated oven at 180 °C for 25–30 minutes or until a skewer comes out clean when tested. Cool for 10 minutes in the cake pan before turning out onto a cooling rack.

For the icing, place the butter, water and castor sugar into a saucepan and melt over a gentle heat. Sift the icing sugar and cocoa powder and stir into the melted butter mixture. Mix well. Cool until starting to thicken, then beat with a wooden spoon and spread over the cooled cake. Decorate with chocolate-dipped pecan nuts if desired.

Chocolate fudge cake

CHOCOLATE GANACHE CAKE

The ultimate in chocolate cakes containing cocoa, dark chocolate and cream.

200 ml cake flour

50 ml cocoa powder

250 ml white sugar

15 ml baking powder

pinch of salt

125 ml sunflower oil

125 ml water

5 ml vanilla essence

4 extra-large eggs, separated

100 g dark chocolate, grated

CHOCOLATE GANACHE

100 g dark chocolate, broken into pieces

50 ml fresh cream

fresh strawberries to decorate (optional)

For the cake, sift the flour, cocoa powder, sugar, baking powder and salt into a mixing bowl. Beat in the oil, water, vanilla essence, egg yolks and grated chocolate until just combined. In a separate bowl, whisk the egg whites until stiff, then fold into the flour mixture. Pour the cake batter into a 22 cm springform pan lined then sprayed with non-stick cooking spray. Bake in a preheated oven at 180 °C for about 40 minutes, until a skewer comes out clean when tested. Remove the cake from the oven and allow to cool in the pan for 15 minutes. Remove and place on a cooling rack to cool completely.

For the ganache, place the chocolate and cream into a small heatproof dish and microwave on medium for 2–3 minutes, until melted. Stir well until smooth. Cool to the correct consistency to coat the cake. Decorate with fresh strawberries if desired.

Chocolate ganache cake

WHITE CHOCOLATE GANACHE CAKE

*Baking with white chocolate can be tricky. For success, ensure you use
the cooking chocolate and not the eating variety.*

100 g white cooking chocolate, broken into pieces
250 ml milk
150 g butter
375 ml castor sugar
500 ml cake flour
7.5 ml baking powder
2 extra-large eggs
5 ml vanilla essence

WHITE CHOCOLATE GANACHE

100 g white cooking chocolate, broken into pieces
50 ml fresh cream
30 g butter
5 ml vanilla essence
100 ml icing sugar

For the cake, combine the chocolate, milk, butter and castor sugar in a saucepan over low heat and stir until the mixture is melted and smooth. Sift the flour and baking powder into a bowl. Add the eggs, vanilla essence and chocolate mixture and whisk until smooth. Pour the mixture into a 22 cm springform pan, lined then sprayed with non-stick cooking spray, and bake in a preheated oven at 160 °C for 40–50 minutes or until a skewer comes out clean when tested. Cool in the pan for about 15 minutes before turning out onto a cooling rack.

For the ganache, heat the chocolate, cream and butter in the microwave on medium for 2–3 minutes, or in a bowl over boiling water, until the chocolate has melted. Add the vanilla essence and mix well. Sift in the icing sugar and beat well. If the mixture is still warm, place it in the fridge to cool until it is the right consistency to coat the cake.

White chocolate ganache cake

CAKES

RED VELVET CAKE

500 ml flour
7.5 ml bicarbonate of soda
pinch of salt
250 ml buttermilk
15 ml white vinegar
5 ml vanilla essence
2 extra-large eggs
30 ml cocoa powder
30 ml red food colouring
180 g butter, softened
375 ml sugar

ICING
125 g butter, softened
250 g thick cream cheese, softened
5 ml vanilla essence
500 ml icing sugar, sifted

For the cake, sift the flour, bicarbonate of soda and salt into a mixing bowl. In a separate bowl, whisk the buttermilk, vinegar, vanilla essence and eggs. Combine the cocoa powder with the food colouring in another small bowl and mix to form a paste. Separately, cream the butter and sugar until fluffy. Add the flour and buttermilk mixtures alternately, beating after each addition. Add the cocoa mixture and beat well. Divide the batter between two 20 cm cake pans sprayed with non-stick cooking spray. Bake in a preheated oven at 180 °C for 25–30 minutes or until a skewer comes out clean when tested. Allow to cool in the pans before turning the cakes out onto cooling racks.

For the icing, cream the butter and cream cheese until smooth and fluffy. Add the vanilla essence and the icing sugar to the mixture. Beat until smooth. Use a third of the icing to sandwich the cake layers together, then spread the remaining icing on the top and sides.

Red velvet cake

COLA-CHOCOLATE CAKE

410 ml flour

7 ml baking powder

3 ml bicarbonate of soda

60 ml cocoa powder

375 ml castor sugar

250 g butter

200 ml cola drink

80 ml milk

2 eggs, beaten

5 ml vanilla essence

FUDGE ICING

50 g butter

50 ml castor sugar

30 ml water

250 ml icing sugar

45 ml cocoa powder

For the cake, sift the flour, baking powder, bicarbonate of soda and cocoa powder into a large mixing bowl. Stir in the sugar. In a saucepan, heat the butter and cola over a low heat until melted. Add to the dry ingredients and mix well. Add the milk, eggs and vanilla essence and mix until smooth. Spoon the mixture into a deep 23 cm ring pan, lined with greaseproof paper and sprayed with non-stick cooking spray. Bake in a preheated oven at 180 °C for 40 minutes or until a skewer comes out clean when tested. Allow to cool in the pan for 15 minutes before turning out onto a cooling rack to cool completely.

For the icing, combine the butter, castor sugar and water in a small saucepan and melt over a gentle heat. In a bowl, sift the icing sugar and cocoa powder and stir into the melted butter mixture. Mix well. Cool until starting to thicken, then beat with a wooden spoon and spread over the cooled cake.

Cola-chocolate cake

CUPCAKES

125 g butter
250 ml castor sugar
2 eggs
500 ml flour
7 ml baking powder
150–180 ml milk
5 ml vanilla essence

BUTTER ICING
100 g butter
500 ml icing sugar, sifted
30–40 ml milk
5 ml vanilla essence

GLACÉ ICING
500 ml icing sugar
water to mix
food colouring

For the cupcakes, cream the butter and sugar until the mixture is light and fluffy. Add the eggs, one at a time, beating well after each addition. Sift the flour and baking powder and add to the creamed mixture alternately with the milk and vanilla essence, adding enough milk to make a soft dropping consistency. Mix until combined.

Spoon into paper-lined muffin pans, filling each to between a half and three-quarters full, depending on how big you want your cupcakes to be. Bake in a preheated oven at 180 °C for 15–20 minutes until light golden brown. Cool on a cooling rack and ice as desired, with either the butter or the glacé icing.

For the butter icing, cream the butter until soft. Add the icing sugar. Add enough milk to make a soft spreading consistency. Mix in the vanilla essence and spread over the cupcakes.

For the glacé icing, sift the icing sugar and mix it with enough water to make a stiff consistency. Colour as desired with a few drops of food colouring and spread over the cupcakes. Decorate as desired.
MAKES 18

Cupcakes

BISCUITS
AND RUSKS

CHOCOLATE CHIP COOKIES

125 g butter

300 ml light brown sugar

1 extra-large egg

5 ml vanilla essence

350 ml cake flour, sifted

5 ml bicarbonate of soda

125 ml raisins

100 g pecan nuts, chopped

250 ml chocolate chips

Cream the butter and sugar well. Beat in the egg and vanilla essence. Add the flour and bicarbonate of soda and mix well. Stir in the raisins, nuts and chocolate chips. Place tablespoonfuls of dough onto a baking sheet sprayed with non-stick cooking spray and flatten slightly. Bake in a preheated oven at 180 °C for 15–20 minutes. **MAKES 24**

COCONUT CRISPIE BISCUITS

This recipe is a great cookie jar filler.

250 g butter

500 ml white sugar

2 extra-large eggs

5 ml vanilla essence

50 ml peanut butter

500 ml cake flour

5 ml baking powder

pinch of salt

5 ml bicarbonate of soda

500 ml desiccated coconut

500 ml rolled oats

500 ml Rice Krispies®

Cream the butter and sugar together until light and fluffy. Add the eggs, one at a time, beating well after each addition. Add the vanilla essence and peanut butter. In a separate bowl, sift the flour, baking powder, salt and bicarbonate of soda together, then add to the creamed mixture. Stir in the coconut, oats and Rice Krispies®. Place teaspoonfuls of the mixture onto greased baking sheets and flatten slightly with a fork. Bake in a preheated oven at 180 °C for 12–15 minutes or until golden brown. Leave to cool for a few minutes, then transfer to a cooling rack. **MAKES ABOUT 70**

Chocolate chip cookies

BISCUITS AND RUSKS

CHOCOLATE-COFFEE CRINKLES

80 g butter
250 ml light brown sugar
125 ml cocoa powder
20 ml instant coffee granules
5 ml bicarbonate of soda
5 ml ground cinnamon
2 extra-large egg whites
80 ml plain yoghurt
375 ml cake flour
extra white sugar

Cream the butter well. Add the sugar, cocoa powder, coffee granules, bicarbonate of soda and cinnamon and mix well. Add the egg whites and yoghurt and mix. Mix in the flour to make a soft dough. Roll into balls about the size of a walnut and drop into granulated sugar to coat. Place the balls about 2 cm apart onto a baking sheet sprayed with non-stick cooking spray and bake in a preheated oven at 180 °C for 8–10 minutes. The biscuits will flatten slightly during baking, giving them a crinkled look. **MAKES 36**

PEANUT BUTTER BISCUITS

A perennial favourite and good for lunchboxes too.

125 g butter
125 ml white sugar
125 ml light brown sugar
125 ml peanut butter
1 extra-large egg
5 ml vanilla essence
400 ml cake flour, sifted
5 ml baking powder
2.5 ml bicarbonate of soda
extra white sugar

Cream together the butter and sugars, add the peanut butter and mix well. Beat in the egg and vanilla essence. Add the flour, baking powder and bicarbonate of soda to form a dough. Roll into balls the size of a walnut and toss them in some sugar. Place on a baking sheet sprayed with non-stick cooking spray and flatten slightly with your fingers. Bake in a preheated oven at 180 °C for 10–15 minutes. **MAKES 24**

Chocolate-coffee crinkles

BIG BATCH BISCUITS

A wonderful recipe that, with the addition of a couple of extra ingredients, can be turned into a myriad variations. Simple to make and handy, as the dough can be kept in the freezer for unexpected guests. It is very important to chill the dough for a couple of hours before using. For added luxury, dip baked biscuits in melted chocolate (place on wax or baking paper to set).

500 g butter, softened
500 ml icing sugar, sifted
5 x 250 ml cake flour
10 ml baking powder
pinch of salt
castor sugar for sprinkling

Combine the butter and icing sugar in a large mixing bowl and, using an electric beater, beat until light and creamy. Sift the flour, baking powder and salt and gradually add to the creamed mixture, mixing well to form a workable biscuit dough. The dough should be firm but not sticky. Divide the mixture into three parts and add the variation of your choice (see below). Roll each piece of dough into a sausage shape, about 4 cm in diameter and 25 cm long. Wrap in clingfilm and chill in the fridge for several hours or overnight (or freeze). Once chilled, slice the dough into 1 cm thick rounds and place on a lightly greased baking sheet. Sprinkle each biscuit lightly with castor sugar. Bake in a preheated oven at 180 °C for 12–15 minutes until the biscuits are pale golden brown. Place on cooling racks to cool completely before packing into airtight containers. **MAKES 70**

VARIATIONS
almond biscuits
Add 125 ml ground almonds and 3 ml almond essence to one portion of raw basic biscuit dough.

cherry biscuits
Add 80 ml chopped glacé cherries to one portion of raw basic biscuit dough.

choc chip biscuits
Add 60 ml chocolate chips to one portion of raw basic biscuit dough.

currant biscuits
Add 60 ml currants to one portion of raw basic biscuit dough.

ginger biscuits
Add 5-10 ml ground ginger and 50 ml finely chopped preserved ginger to one portion of raw basic biscuit dough.

pecan nut biscuits
Add 125 ml chopped pecan nuts to one portion of raw basic biscuit dough.

BISCUITS AND RUSKS

ICED GINGER BISCUITS

500 ml cake flour

250 ml soft brown sugar

2.5 ml bicarbonate of soda

15 ml ground ginger

125 g butter, cubed

1 extra-large egg

15 ml golden syrup

white sugar for topping

GLACÉ ICING

250 ml icing sugar, sifted

a little water to mix

crystallized ginger, cut into small pieces

For the biscuits, place the flour, brown sugar, bicarbonate of soda and ginger in the bowl of a food processor. Add the butter and process until the mixture resembles fine breadcrumbs. Lightly beat the egg and syrup together, then add this to the dry ingredients. Process until a firm dough is formed. Take small spoonfuls of dough and roll into walnut-sized balls. Place on a baking sheet sprayed with non-stick cooking spray. Lightly grease the base of a drinking glass with butter and press into the white sugar. Press the glass lightly on top of the biscuits to flatten. Repeat with butter and sugar when necessary. Bake in a preheated oven at 160 °C for 15–20 minutes. Remove from the baking sheet and cool on a cooling rack.

For the icing, mix the icing sugar with just enough water to achieve a thick spreadable consistency. Spread a little icing on each cooled biscuit and top with pieces of crystallized ginger. MAKES 30–40

BISCUITS AND RUSKS

ESPRESSO BISCUITS

These biscuits have a rich coffee flavour.

250 g butter
250 ml icing sugar
15 ml instant espresso coffee granules
30 ml ground espresso beans
30 ml hot water
625 ml cake flour
melted chocolate to decorate (optional)

Using an electric mixer, cream the butter and icing sugar. Dissolve the coffee granules and ground beans in the hot water and cool. Add to the creamed mixture together with the flour and mix well to form a dough. Roll out to about 5 mm thick on a lightly floured surface and cut out with a round 4 cm diameter biscuit cutter. Place on a baking sheet sprayed with non-stick cooking spray and bake in a preheated oven at 180 °C for 10–15 minutes until golden. When completely cool, drizzle with melted chocolate if desired. MAKES 36

JAPANESE OAT CRISPS

200 g butter
375 ml white sugar
250 ml rolled oats
500 ml cake flour
5 ml bicarbonate of soda
1 extra-large egg, lightly beaten

Melt the butter. Combine the sugar, oats, flour and bicarbonate of soda in a mixing bowl. Add the beaten egg and melted butter and mix well. Roll the dough into walnut-sized balls and place on a baking sheet sprayed with non-stick cooking spray. Flatten slightly with your fingers, then bake in a preheated oven at 180 °C for 10–15 minutes until golden and crisp. Cool on the baking sheet. MAKES 36

Espresso biscuits

MELTING MOMENTS

The custard powder gives these biscuits an appetizing colour.

200 g butter
125 ml icing sugar, sifted
5 ml vanilla essence
125 ml custard powder
375 ml cake flour

Cream the butter and icing sugar well. Add the vanilla essence and beat well. Mix in the remaining ingredients to form a dough. Form into walnut-sized balls and arrange on a baking sheet sprayed with non-stick cooking spray. Flatten with a fork. Bake in a preheated oven at 180 °C for 10–15 minutes until pale gold in colour. MAKES 24

SHORTBREAD HEARTS

200 g butter
125 ml castor sugar
185 ml cornflour
375 ml cake flour
extra castor sugar

Cream the butter until soft. Add the castor sugar, cornflour and flour and mix until the dough forms a smooth ball. Roll out on a lightly floured surface and cut out with a heart-shaped cutter. Place on a baking sheet sprayed with non-stick cooking spray and bake in a preheated oven at 180 °C for 15–20 minutes until pale gold in colour. Remove from the oven and sprinkle with extra castor sugar while still warm. MAKES 24

Melting moments

BISCUITS AND RUSKS

CHRISTMAS COOKIES

250 g butter	5 ml bicarbonate of soda
300 ml light brown sugar	10 ml ground cinnamon
2 extra-large eggs	10 ml ground mixed spice
5 ml vanilla essence	125 ml chopped glacé cherries
600 ml cake flour	250 ml dried fruitcake mix
5 ml baking powder	50 g pecan nuts, chopped

Cream the butter and sugar until light and fluffy. Add the eggs and vanilla essence and mix well. Sift the flour, baking powder, bicarbonate of soda and spices, then add this to the creamed mixture. Mix in the cherries, fruit mix and nuts. Roll the dough into golf ball-sized balls and place on a baking sheet sprayed with non-stick cooking spray. Flatten slightly. Bake in a preheated oven at 180 °C for 15–20 minutes until golden brown. Cool on the baking sheet, then store in an airtight container. If desired, drizzle the biscuits with glacé icing made from 250 ml icing sugar mixed with a little water to make a runny consistency. MAKES 36

CHRISTMAS BISCOTTI

Biscotti is the Italian word for biscuit. Great to dunk in coffee, here is a lovely fruit and nut variety.

500 ml cake flour	50 g dates, pitted and chopped
300 ml castor sugar	75 g pistachio nuts, shelled
10 ml baking powder	100 g blanched almonds, roughly chopped
80 ml sultanas	grated rind of 1 lemon
80 ml chopped glacé cherries	3 extra-large eggs

Sift the flour, castor sugar and baking powder into a bowl. Add all the fruit, all the nuts and the lemon rind and mix well. Add the eggs and mix well. Using well-floured hands, shape the mixture into two slightly flattened logs about 20 cm in length. Place on a paper-lined baking sheet and bake in a preheated oven at 180 °C for 20–30 minutes. Remove and leave to stand for 10 minutes. Cut into 1 cm thick slices and return to the baking sheet. Reduce the oven temperature to 140 °C and bake for another 10–12 minutes, turning halfway through the baking time, until pale gold in colour. Remove and cool. **MAKES ABOUT 30**

VARIATION
cappuccino biscotti
Remove the sultanas, cherries, dates, pistachio nuts and lemon rind from the recipe and add 30 ml coffee powder dissolved in 15 ml boiling water (cooled) to the eggs and add to the dry ingredients.

Christmas cookies

BISCUITS AND RUSKS

BUTTERMILK RUSKS

An electric carving knife is great for cutting evenly shaped rusks.

1.5 kg self-raising flour

5 ml salt

500 g butter, cut into cubes

750 ml white sugar

2 extra-large eggs

750 ml buttermilk

Sift the flour and salt into a large mixing bowl. Rub in the butter and add the sugar. In a separate bowl, combine the eggs and buttermilk, then mix this into the flour. Press the mixture into a 40 x 30 x 5 cm deep oven pan sprayed with non-stick cooking spray and bake in a preheated oven at 180 °C for 1 hour. Turn out and cool. Cut into fingers and return to the oven at 70 °C to dry out for 4–5 hours or overnight. **MAKES 60**

HEALTH RUSKS

1 kg self-raising flour

5 ml salt

15 ml baking powder

125 g digestive bran

200 g All-Bran® cereal

375 ml light brown sugar

250 ml raisins

100 g pecan nuts, chopped

500 g butter

2 extra-large eggs

500 ml buttermilk

Place all the dry ingredients in a large mixing bowl and mix well. Melt the butter and combine with the eggs and buttermilk. Add this to the dry ingredients and mix to form a stiff dough. Press the dough into a 40 x 30 x 5 cm deep oven pan sprayed with non-stick cooking spray and bake in a preheated oven at 160 °C for 1 hour. Remove and cool. Cut into pieces, place on a baking sheet and return to the oven at 70 °C to dry out overnight. **MAKES 40–50**

Buttermilk rusks

BISCUITS AND RUSKS

FRUIT AND NUT RUSKS

6 x 250 ml self-raising flour

5 ml salt

10 ml baking powder

500 ml toasted muesli

125 ml sunflower seeds

100 g pecan nuts, chopped

125 ml desiccated coconut

500 ml All-Bran® cereal

125 ml raisins

500 ml light brown sugar

1 apple, peeled and grated

2 extra-large eggs

500 g butter, melted

500 ml buttermilk

Combine all the dry ingredients in a large bowl. Add the apple. In a separate bowl, mix the eggs, butter and buttermilk together and pour into the dry ingredients. Mix well to form a stiff dough. Press the dough into a 40 x 30 x 5 cm deep oven pan sprayed with non-stick cooking spray. Bake in a preheated oven at 180 °C for 50–60 minutes. Cool slightly and turn onto a cooling rack to cool before cutting into fingers. Arrange the rusks on a baking sheet and dry out in the oven at 70 °C overnight. Store in an airtight container. **MAKES 40–50**

Fruit and nut rusks

LOAVES AND TRAY BAKES

GINGERBREAD

Not many can resist the temptation of a slice of fragrant and spicy gingerbread.

125 g butter	5 ml vanilla essence
185 ml light brown sugar	500 ml self-raising flour
125 ml treacle or molasses	7.5 ml ground ginger
125 ml golden or ginger syrup	5 ml ground cinnamon
2 extra-large eggs	5 ml ground mixed spice
175 ml thick plain yoghurt	2.5 ml grated nutmeg
10 ml peeled and finely grated fresh ginger	pinch of ground cloves

Combine the butter, sugar, treacle and syrup in the bowl of an electric mixer and beat together for 2–3 minutes. Add the eggs, one at a time, beating well after each addition. Add the yoghurt, fresh ginger and vanilla essence. Sift the flour and spices together and fold into the creamed mixture. Pour the batter into a 24 x 10 cm loaf pan sprayed with non-stick cooking spray and bake in a preheated oven at 170 °C for 40–50 minutes. The loaf will develop characteristic cracks as it bakes. **MAKES 1 LOAF**

MOIST BANANA-DATE LOAF

This quick-and-easy loaf, which is delicious spread with butter, is a good way to use up bananas that are past their sell-by date. Replace the dates with two extra bananas for a banana loaf.

500 ml self-raising flour, sifted

125 ml caramel brown sugar

250 g dates, pitted and chopped

125 g butter, softened

325 ml milk

2 extra-large eggs, beaten

3 large ripe bananas, mashed

Combine the flour, sugar and dates in a mixing bowl. Beat in the butter, milk, eggs and bananas and mix until well combined. Pour the batter into a 23 x 13 cm loaf pan sprayed with non-stick cooking spray. Bake in a preheated oven at 170 °C for 50–60 minutes. **MAKES 1 LARGE LOAF**

Gingerbread

NUTTY CINNAMON PICNIC BAKE

Made in a purchased foil container, this bake is perfectly portable.

285 ml white sugar

50 g whole peeled almonds, chopped

10 ml ground cinnamon

125 g butter

2 extra-large eggs

5 ml vanilla essence

15 ml lemon juice

500 ml cake flour

3 ml baking powder

3 ml bicarbonate of soda

pinch of salt

250 ml sour cream

Combine 35 ml of the sugar with the almonds and cinnamon and set aside. In a separate bowl, cream the butter and remaining sugar until light and fluffy. Add the eggs, vanilla essence and lemon juice. Sift the flour, baking powder, bicarbonate of soda and salt together, then add the flour mixture to the creamed mixture alternately with the sour cream. Spray a 24 x 16 cm rectangular foil container with non-stick cooking spray, or use two smaller foil loaf pans. Pour the batter into the container. Sprinkle the top evenly with the reserved sugar and nut mixture. Place in a preheated oven at 180 °C for 45 minutes. Cool and serve from the container. **MAKES 1 TRAY BAKE OR 2 SMALL LOAVES**

Nutty cinnamon picnic bake

LOAVES AND TRAY BAKES

BANANA-HONEYCOMB TEA BREAD

For a plain banana bread, the Crunchie™ can be omitted.

100 g butter

125 ml castor sugar

2 extra-large eggs

4–6 ripe bananas, mashed (should make about 375 ml)

80 ml buttermilk

500 ml cake flour, sifted

10 ml baking powder, sifted

2 x 40 g Crunchie™ bars, chopped or 70 g honeycomb, chopped

Cream the butter and castor sugar. Add the eggs and bananas and mix well. Add the buttermilk and stir until well combined. Add the flour and baking powder and mix well. Add the Crunchie™ or honeycomb and stir until combined. Spoon the batter into a 23 x 13 cm loaf pan lined then sprayed with non-stick cooking spray and bake in a preheated oven at 180 °C for 50–60 minutes. Turn out onto a rack and cool. Top with extra chopped Crunchie™ if desired. **MAKES 1 LOAF**

LOW-FAT TEA LOAF

Virtually fat free, bar the oil and eggs, the baked loaves freeze very well. For a more decadent, delicious option, serve spread with butter.

2 tea bags — 4 x 250 ml cake flour

500 ml boiling water — 20 ml baking powder

500 g dried fruitcake mix — 5 ml ground cinnamon

30 ml sunflower oil — 5 ml ground mixed spice

2 extra-large eggs — 5 ml vanilla essence

375 ml caramel brown sugar

Immerse the tea bags in the boiling water in a large mixing bowl until you have a strong brew. Soak the fruitcake mix in the tea together with the tea bags overnight. Discard the tea bags, and add the oil, eggs and sugar to the tea mixture. Mix well. Sift the flour, baking powder and spices together, then add to the tea mixture and mix well. Add the vanilla essence. Spoon the batter into two 22 x 12 cm loaf pans lined with baking paper and sprayed with non-stick cooking spray. Bake in a preheated oven at 160 °C for 60–70 minutes. Test by piercing with a toothpick in the centres. Leave to cool in the pans before transferring to a rack to cool completely. **MAKES 2 LOAVES**

Banana-honeycomb tea bread

ONE-BOWL CITRUS LOAF

Easy as pie and a great way to introduce children to baking. You only need one bowl and a wooden spoon so there's very little washing up too! If preferred, leave out the citrus and add 5 ml vanilla essence for a plain vanilla loaf.

125 g butter, softened
375 ml cake flour
190 ml white sugar
10 ml baking powder
2 extra-large eggs
10–15 ml finely grated lemon or orange rind
125 ml milk

GLACÉ ICING
250 ml icing sugar, sifted
20 ml lemon or orange juice
a little hot water
lemon or orange zest to decorate

For the loaf, combine all the loaf ingredients in a mixing bowl and mix with a wooden spoon until you have a smooth batter. Pour the batter into a 23 x 12 cm loaf pan sprayed with non-stick cooking spray. Bake in a preheated oven at 180 °C for 40–60 minutes. Remove and cool completely.

For the icing, combine the icing sugar, lemon or orange juice and a little hot water until you have a thick but still runny icing. Pour the icing over the cooled loaf and decorate with lemon or orange zest.

MAKES 1 LOAF

One-bowl citrus loaf

LOAVES AND TRAY BAKES

COCONUT BATTER LOAF

This loaf is good on its own or toasted and served with preserves.

625 ml flour

12.5 ml baking powder

pinch of salt

5 ml ground cinnamon

250 ml sugar

125 g shredded coconut (you can use desiccated coconut)

2 extra-large eggs

300 ml milk

60 g butter, melted

In a large mixing bowl, sift together the flour, baking powder, salt and cinnamon. Add the sugar and coconut. In a separate bowl, beat together the eggs, milk and melted butter and add to the dry ingredients. Mix well. Pour the batter into a well-greased 20 cm loaf pan and bake at 180 °C for 60 minutes. Leave to cool in the pan for 5 minutes before turning out onto a wire rack to cool completely. **MAKES 1 LOAF**

MUESLI LOAF

A wholesome, nutty seed loaf that is delicious sliced and spread with butter. Better still, toast it and spread with butter while still warm.

250 ml wholewheat flour	500 ml buttermilk or thick plain yoghurt
250 ml self-raising flour	60 ml runny honey
250 ml raw (untoasted) muesli	50 ml sunflower seeds
125 ml raisins or sultanas	50 ml linseed
2.5 ml salt	50 ml sesame seeds
5 ml bicarbonate of soda	100 g pecan nuts or walnuts, crushed

Combine both flours, the muesli, raisins and salt in a large mixing bowl. In a separate bowl, combine the bicarbonate of soda, buttermilk and honey, then add this to the dry ingredients along with all the seeds and the nuts. Spoon the batter into a 22 x 12 cm loaf pan sprayed with non-stick cooking spray and level the top. Bake in a preheated oven at 170 °C for 60–70 minutes. Cool in the pan for about 5 minutes before transferring to a cooling rack. **MAKES 1 LOAF**

Coconut batter loaf

APPLE AND CHEESE LOAF

125 g butter, softened

150 ml castor sugar

2 extra-large eggs

500 ml cake flour, sifted

5 ml baking powder

pinch of grated nutmeg

5 ml salt

80 ml buttermilk

250 ml grated mature cheddar cheese

50 g walnuts or pecan nuts, chopped

2 large Granny Smith apples, peeled and grated
and tossed in 15 ml lemon juice

Using an electric hand beater, cream together the butter and castor sugar until light and fluffy. Add the eggs, one at a time, beating well after each addition, then add the flour, baking powder, nutmeg, salt and enough buttermilk to make a thick batter. Fold in the cheese, nuts and apple and mix well. Pour the batter into a 22 x 12 cm loaf pan (or use mini loaf pans) sprayed with non-stick cooking spray. Bake in a preheated oven at 160 °C for 60–70 minutes – or 20–30 minutes if using mini loaf pans – until the loaf is well risen and firm. Leave to cool in the pan for 5 minutes before turning out onto a wire rack to cool completely. **MAKES 1 LOAF OR 8 MINI LOAVES**

STICKY GINGER TRAY BAKE

This makes a large, moist gingerbread that cuts into perfect squares and will feed a crowd. If desired, omit the icing, cut into squares and dust with icing sugar.

300 ml golden syrup

300 ml black treacle

250 ml treacle brown sugar

200 g butter

900 ml self-raising flour, sifted

10 ml ground mixed spice

10 ml ground ginger

4 extra-large eggs, lightly beaten

ICING

500 ml icing sugar, sifted

warm water to mix

100 g preserved ginger, syrup drained
and reserved, finely chopped

For the gingerbread, combine the syrup, treacle, sugar and butter in a large microwave-proof mixing bowl and heat on medium for 2–3 minutes until the butter has melted. Remove and stir in the flour and spices. Add the eggs and beat until smooth; the consistency will be quite runny. Pour the mixture into a 40 x 30 x 5 cm deep oven pan sprayed with non-stick cooking spray and bake in a preheated oven at 170 °C for 45 minutes. It is cooked when the gingerbread pulls away from the sides of the pan. Cool.

For the icing, place the icing sugar in a bowl and add a little water at a time to make a runny icing. Add a little of the reserved ginger syrup. Pour over the cooled tray bake and sprinkle over the chopped preserved ginger. Leave to set, then cut into squares. **MAKES 30 SQUARES**

Apple and cheese loaf

LOAVES AND TRAY BAKES

CHELSEA TRAY BAKE

Imagine a whole trayful of sinful Chelsea buns without having to use yeast. This is a great way for quickly making up a quantity for a crowd and is delicious served warm with coffee.

DOUGH
750 ml self-raising flour, sifted
125 g butter
150–175 ml milk
melted butter for brushing

FILLING
75 g dried fruitcake mix
100 g pecan nuts, chopped
125 ml caramel brown sugar
7.5 ml ground cinnamon
2.5 ml ground cloves
50 g butter, melted

ICING
250 ml icing sugar
warm water to mix
squeeze of lemon juice

For the dough, place the flour and butter in the bowl of a food processor and process until the mixture resembles breadcrumbs. With the machine running, add just enough milk until the mixture forms a ball, then stop immediately. Roll out the dough into a large rectangle on a lightly floured surface. Brush with melted butter.

For the filling, combine the fruitcake mix, nuts, sugar and spices and spread over the dough. Sprinkle over the melted butter. Roll up the dough like a swiss roll and cut into 12 equal slices. Spray a 25 cm square pan with non-stick cooking spray and arrange the slices close together, with the cut sides uppermost. Leave to stand for 5 minutes. Bake in a preheated oven at 180 °C for 30–40 minutes. Cool in the pan.

For the icing, mix together the icing sugar, a little water and the lemon juice to make a runny icing. Drizzle over the Chelsea buns. **MAKES 12**

Chelsea tray bake

FESTIVE MINCEMEAT BAKE

Makes a change from mince pies, and these are quicker to make.

BASE
4 x 250 ml cake flour

15 ml baking powder

pinch of salt

5 ml ground mixed spice

7.5 ml ground cinnamon

400 ml icing sugar, sifted

250 g butter, softened

2 extra-large eggs

FILLING
1 x 400 g jar fruit mincemeat

1 large Granny Smith apple, peeled, cored and grated

rind and juice of 1 lemon

50 g pecan nuts or almonds, chopped

icing sugar for dusting

For the base, sift the flour, baking powder, salt, spices and icing sugar into the bowl of a food processor. Add the butter and eggs and process until the mixture forms a ball. Press three-quarters of the dough onto the base of a large baking sheet sprayed with non-stick cooking spray. Set the leftover dough aside in the fridge, covered, while preparing the filling.

For the filling, combine the mincemeat, apple, lemon rind and juice and nuts. Spread evenly over the dough base, then grate the reserved dough over the top. Bake in a preheated oven at 160 °C for 40–50 minutes until golden brown and cooked through. Remove from the oven and, while still warm, dust liberally with icing sugar. Cut into squares. **MAKES 48 SQUARES**

COCKEYED CHOCOLATE SQUARES

Looking at this eggless recipe you would be convinced it could not work out. Well it does, and the best part is that it is mixed in the baking pan so there are no extra dishes! To make a larger version, simply double the ingredients and bake in a roasting pan.

375 ml cake flour

250 ml castor sugar

45 ml cocoa powder

5 ml baking powder

2.5 ml salt

5 ml vanilla essence

75 ml sunflower oil

15 ml white vinegar

250 ml cold water

chocolate nut spread to decorate (optional)

Spray a 27 x 18 cm cake pan with non-stick cooking spray. Sift all the dry ingredients directly into the pan. Make three indentations in the mixture. In one hole, pour in the vanilla essence, add the oil to the second hole and the vinegar to the third. Pour over the cold water and mix with a spatula until just combined. Bake in a preheated oven at 180 °C for 30 minutes. Cool on a wire rack and, if desired, spread the top with warmed chocolate nut spread. **MAKES 16 SQUARES**

LOAVES AND TRAY BAKES

TOFFEE SQUARES

It really is just like biting into a yummy toffee, only softer.

BISCUIT BASE AND TOPPING
250 g butter, softened
180 ml white sugar
10 ml instant coffee granules, dissolved in a dash of hot water
600 ml cake flour
5 ml baking powder

TOFFEE FILLING
1 x 397 g can condensed milk
45 ml golden syrup
45 g butter
45 ml white sugar

For the base and topping, cream the butter and sugar until light and creamy. Beat in the coffee. Sift the flour and baking powder together and add to the creamed mixture. Mix well until the mixture forms a soft dough. Press two-thirds of the dough into a 30 x 23 cm baking sheet sprayed with non-stick cooking spray. Wrap the remaining dough in clingfilm and chill in the freezer.

For the filling, combine the condensed milk, syrup, butter and sugar in a saucepan and heat over low heat until the sugar dissolves. Bring to the boil and cook for about 12 minutes, stirring constantly, until the mixture is thick and golden brown. Spread the toffee mixture over the base. Grate the reserved dough over the toffee and bake in a preheated oven at 180 °C for 25–30 minutes. Cool in the pan, then cut into squares. **MAKES 24 SQUARES**

Toffee squares

DECADENTLY RICH COFFEE SHOP BROWNIES

You can't have recipes for tray bakes and not include brownies. For a less expensive version,
simply leave out the roughly chopped white and dark chocolate.

200 g dark chocolate

200 g butter

4 extra-large eggs

250 ml castor sugar

5 ml vanilla essence

330 ml cake flour, sifted

60 ml cocoa powder, sifted

100 g pecan nuts, roughly chopped

100 g white cooking chocolate, roughly chopped

100 g dark chocolate, roughly chopped

sifted icing sugar for dusting (optional)

Melt the dark chocolate and butter in a heatproof bowl over boiling water or use a double boiler. Cool slightly. Using a wire whisk, combine the eggs, castor sugar and vanilla essence and add to the melted chocolate. Mix well. Add the flour and cocoa powder to the chocolate mixture with the chopped nuts and extra chopped chocolate. Pour the batter into a 30 x 20 cm pan lined with baking paper and sprayed with non-stick cooking spray. Bake in a preheated oven at 180 °C for 30–40 minutes. Cool in the pan. Remove, cut into squares and dust with icing sugar if desired. **MAKES 12 SQUARES**

Decadently rich coffee shop brownies

INDEX

Page numbers in bold type indicate photographs.

Published in 2010 by Struik Lifestyle
(an imprint of Random House Struik (Pty) Ltd)
Company Reg. No. 1966/003153/07
80 McKenzie Street, Cape Town 8001
PO Box 1144, Cape Town, 8000, South Africa

First published in 2005 by Struik Publishers
Reprinted in 2006
Second edition published by Struik Lifestyle in 2010

PUBLISHER: Linda de Villiers
MANAGING EDITOR: Cecilia Barfield
EDITORS: Joy Clack (1st ed)
and Bronwen Leak (2nd ed)
DESIGNER: Beverley Dodd
PHOTOGRAPHER: C&D Heierli Photography
STYLIST: Lisa Clark
STYLIST'S ASSISTANTS: Katherine Freemantle
and Yvette Pascoe

Reproduction: Hirt & Carter Cape (Pty) Ltd
Printing and binding: Craft Print International Ltd

ISBN 978-1-77007-863-5

www.imagesofafrica.co.za
IMAGES OF AFRICA
PHOTO LIBRARY

Over 40 000 unique African images available
to purchase from our image bank at
www.imagesofafrica.co.za

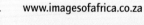